# Heaven
## *on* Earth

McDougal & Associates
Servants of Christ and Stewards of the
Mysteries of God

# Heaven *on* Earth

by

## Dr. Abiola Idowu

McDougal & Associates is dedicated to spreading the Gospel
of the Lord Jesus Christ to as many people as possible in the
shortest time possible.

Published by:

McDougal & Associates
18896 Greenwell Springs Road
Greenwell Springs, LA 70739
www,ThePublishedWord.com

ISBN: 978-1-950398-62-1

Printed on demand in the U.S., the U.K., Australia and the UAE
For Worldwide Distribution

# DEDICATION

This book is dedicated to all the saints of God who desire to live in the fullness of His plan for their lives on this Earth and experience the manifestation of His glory. You are blessed.

# Contents

Introduction ................................................................................. 11

**Part I: The Foundation for Establishing Heaven on Earth ........ 15**

1. What Is Heaven on Earth? ......................................................... 17

2. What Did Jesus Reveal about Heaven on Earth? ................... 25

3. What Did Jesus Do to Bring About Heaven on Earth? ......... 31

4. What Is the New Eden? .............................................................. 41

5. What Does It Mean to Be Like Jesus? ...................................... 49

6. What Does It Mean to Live in the Light and Speak Light .... 59

7. Why Is It Necessary to Give Voice to Your Promises? .......... 69

8. What Does It Mean to Experience True Peace? ...................... 75

9. Why Is It So Important to Understand the Love of God? .... 85

10. Why Is It So Important to Believe What God Says? .............. 91

11. Why Is It Important to Recognize Jesus as King? .................. 97

12. Why Is the Seed So Important? ............................................... 105

13. Why Is It Important Not to Be Controlled by Money? ....... 119

14. Why Is Giving Such an Important Key to Prosperity? ....... 127

15. Why Is It Important to Recognize the Grace of God? ......... 133

16. Why Is It Important to Understand the Blessing> ............... 141


**Part II: Looking in the Mirror** ...................................................**161**

17. Your Blessing Is Here ............................................................163

18. Changed into the Same Image...........................................187

19. The Promise of the Spirit through Faith ...........................217

20. In Conclusion.........................................................................243


Author Contact Information ................................................255

THY KINGDOM COME,
THY WILL BE DONE IN EARTH,
AS IT IS IN HEAVEN.
— MATTHEW 6:10

IF THE PLACE WHICH THE LORD
THY GOD HATH CHOSEN TO PUT HIS
NAME THERE BE TOO FAR FROM THEE,
THEN THOU SHALT KILL OF THY HERD
AND OF THY FLOCK, WHICH THE
LORD HATH GIVEN THEE, AS I HAVE
COMMANDED THEE, AND THOU SHALT
EAT IN THY GATES WHATSOEVER
THY SOUL LUSTETH AFTER.
— DEUTERONOMY 12:21

# INTRODUCTION

When the intention of a thing is not known, the response is affected, and the potential benefits are aborted. God wants Heaven on the Earth. His intention from Creation was to put man on an Earth that looked like Heaven.

Man was not made like other parts of creation; he was made in the image and likeness of God. The Garden of Eden, the place God prepared for mankind, was a glorious place and is described in the Scriptures in the book of Genesis:

> *And a river went out of Eden to water the garden; and from thence it was parted, and became into four heads. The name of the first is Pison: that is it which compasseth the whole land of Havilah,*

*where there is gold; and the gold of that land is good: there is bdellium and the onyx stone. And the Lord God took the man, and put him into the garden of Eden to dress it and to keep it.*

Genesis 2:10-12 and 15

Then, let's look at the way Heaven is described in Revelation:

*And the building of the wall of it was of jasper: and the city was pure gold, like unto clear glass. And the foundations of the wall of the city were garnished with all manner of precious stones. The first foundation was jasper; the second, sapphire; the third, a chalcedony; the fourth, an emerald; the fifth, sardonyx; the sixth, sardius; the seventh, chrysolite; the eighth, beryl; the ninth, a topaz; the tenth, a chrysoprasus; the eleventh, a jacinth; the twelfth, an amethyst.*

Revelation 21:18-20

It is clear that there is a resemblance here that God brought from Heaven to the original Earth. Jesus, when He walked among men on the Earth, said that we should pray for the Father's will to be done *"in earth as it is in heaven"* (Matthew 6:10). God intended for His will and purposes to be done here on Earth just as it is done in Heaven.

Think about that! There is no sickness and disease in Heaven. There is no lack. There is no oppression, no stagnation, and no failure. So, if God's will is that what is done in Heaven be done here on Earth, then we who are believers in Christ should not be experiencing these things here either.

We know that sin entered, man fell, and Creation was tarnished, but we also know that the Son of God paid the price to redeem mankind and bring back Heaven to Earth. The sooner we understand this, the better life will be for us. We can only enjoy our inheritance when the eyes of our understanding are opened to the truth. And that is what we will attempt to do in this book.

Get ready to take back what belongs to you because of redemption through the cross of Christ. Get ready to walk in your true authority and power. Get ready to manifest the anointing and grace of true sonship.

As you read this book with an open heart, the Holy Spirit will begin to open your eyes to what is already in you, ready to be deployed for the world to enjoy. Join me as we go on an adventure in the world of spiritual exploits and results through Christ Jesus and the provision of our great redemption. Beloved, it is your turn and now is the time to live in *Heaven on Earth*.

*Shalom!*
*Bishop Dr. Abiola Idowu*
*Jacksonville, Florida*

# PART I

# THE FOUNDATIONS FOR EXPERIENCING HEAVEN ON EARTH

CHAPTER 1

# WHAT IS HEAVEN ON EARTH?

*And the LORD God took the man, and*
*put him into the garden of Eden to dress*
*it and to keep it. And the LORD God*
*commanded the man, saying, Of every*
*tree of the garden thou mayest freely*
*eat: but of the tree of the knowledge of*
*good and evil, thou shalt not eat of it: for*
*in the day that thou eatest thereof thou*
*shalt surely die.* Genesis 2:15-17

You are about to see why it should be
impossible for you, as a believer in Jesus
Christ, to fail, why sickness, diseases, and
premature death must never dictate to you.
Jesus Christ was sent from Heaven to Earth
to show us how humanity was intended to

live. He came to reveal the heavenly pattern of living because mankind had been deceived and then desecrated through spiritual death.

What happen in the Garden of Eden was not a physical death at all. If it had been a physical death that God spoke to Adam and Eve about, they would have died immediately when they ate the forbidden fruit. In fact, Adam went on to live for more than 960 years.

So, it was not a physical death. Instead, it was a death that separated men and women from God. They were first dead spiritually (separated from God), and physical death came much later. When Adam and Eve sinned, they immediately died spiritually, and everything that accompanies death came upon their lives.

Suddenly, this otherwise perfect man and woman got sick, they experienced oppression, they suffered poverty, and they began to fail in every sense of the word. It all happened because they were now under a new governmental regime, one whose manifesto was: steal, kill, and destroy:

*The thief cometh not, but for to steal, and to kill, and to destroy: I am come that they might have life, and that they might have it more abundantly.*

John 10:10

Everything this new government devised was being fulfilled, and man seemed powerless to stop it. He could not see the reality of the life God intended anymore because he was disconnected from truth. The only available information was what the enemy fed him through his intellect, and his intellect became the governor of his life.

Suddenly man was feeding on a fallen state of mind. He was intended to live by spiritual discernment, not human intellect. Adam didn't go to the same school as you and I, but we are not nearly as intelligent as he was. He named all the animals on the Earth, and he did it without a notebook, a smart phone or an iPad.

Adam had originally been in position to receive downloads directly from Heaven. The things God thought were the things

Adam thought, for he was one with God. But when Adam sinned and death came, there was a sudden disconnect. Now the only information available to man was what his senses supplied.

Unfortunately for mankind, all their information was now coming from the new lord over their lives, and the purpose of that information was to steal, kill, destroy, and make Adam and Eve and their descendants as miserable as possible.

It was only then that man begin to celebrate educational degrees. He was suddenly so proud of his mental accomplishments. But, because of the Fall, any knowledge man acquired was severely tainted and severely limited. Now, nothing that came from him was perfect. It was all flawed thinking.

Being lied to and being deceived are two very different things. When someone lies to you, you may eventually discover the lie, but when you are deceived, you will spend your life trying to prove to others that you are right ... despite the fact that you are so wrong. This is what has happened to modern society. Over the years, we have been brainwashed by the devil. Whatever your educational qualifications might be and however many people you may know, if you attempt to live in this Earth without Christ, you are deceived.

Revelation tells us:

> *And the great dragon was cast out, that old serpent, called the Devil, and Satan, which deceiveth the whole world: he was cast out into the earth, and his angels were cast out with him.*
>
> Revelation 12:9

I want to show you some things that will change your view completely. What I am about to reveal to you is not what our modern religions have been teaching. The devil has deceived the entire world, and you are not immune to his deceptions. If you are on this Earth, you have been subjected to his lies, for they have affected the population of the entire Earth.

Recently a man died from taking a popular medication that has been available only a few years. The doctors who prescribed this medication to him certainly did not intend to kill him, but everything man does is faulty. Other people who used the same medication were helped by it, but this man was killed by it. When it happened, news reporters stated that anyone who had been adversely affected by this drug should file a claim. But what of those who had already been killed by it? What can they claim? Our world is deceived.

When Jesus came to Earth, He came with information that would show us how Heaven operates, and He wants us to operate on this Earth as if we were in Heaven. He said:

> *Verily, verily, I say unto thee, We speak that we do know, and testify that we have seen; and ye receive not our witness. If I have told you earthly things, and ye believe not, how shall ye believe, if I tell you of heavenly things? And no*

*man hath ascended up to heaven, but he that came down from heaven, even the Son of man which is in heaven.*

John 3:11-13

The devil will do anything to stop you from reading a book like this one and attending a church that preaches the redemption that Jesus Christ purchased for you through His death on Calvary. There will always be very good reasons (but very stupid ones) to keep you from these truths.

I urge you to stand firm. You have not been to Heaven, but Jesus lives there, and He can show you what Heaven is like and what Heaven on Earth would be like and should be like. The most wonderful truth is that you can experience *Heaven on Earth* right here and right now.

# CHAPTER 2

# WHAT DID JESUS REVEAL ABOUT HEAVEN ON EARTH?

*The Spirit of the Lord is upon me, because he hath anointed me to preach the gospel to the poor; he hath sent me to heal the brokenhearted, to preach deliverance to the captives, and recovering of sight to the blind, to set at liberty them that are bruised, to preach the acceptable year of the Lord.*          Luke 4:18-19

While Jesus was here in the flesh, He was living on Earth, but His method of operation was heavenly. Therefore, He never got sick, He was never oppressed, He was never tormented. Everything He put His hands to succeeded because He was operating from a realm that the power of this world cannot hinder.

The important thing to remember is that Jesus was our example. He showed us the intention of Almighty God, that man (humanity) should rule this universe and dominate it. This had been ordained from the beginning of time:

> *And God said, Let us make man in our image, after our likeness: and let them have dominion over the fish of the sea, and over the fowl of the air, and over the cattle, and over all the earth, and over every creeping thing that creepeth upon the earth.* Genesis 1:26

There is nothing in creation that God has not given mankind the ability to dominate. Everything was created to submit to the leadership of mankind on the Earth.

This includes the other planets. Man can stand on the Earth and control the other planets. The only thing God reserved to

Himself was His sovereignty, and I will prove it to you from the Scriptures.

Man (meaning mankind) was created to be in the same class as his Maker. When the Scriptures say that God created man *"in his image and likeness,"* it refers to His class.

If I hold a mirror and look into it, who will I be looking at? Myself, right? If I look in a mirror and see someone other than myself, I know that something is terribly wrong. Well, in the same way that I look in a mirror and see myself, when God looks at you, He sees Himself. You are created in His image and likeness. You are in a class with God.

Think of how powerful Adam was. The moment he "messed up," everything that God had created was plunged into darkness. All the animals and plants suddenly began to act against God's plan, and death took hold of creation. The only thing that was not adversely affected by Adam's sin was the throne of God itself:

> *And almost all things are by the law purged with blood; and without shed-*

*ding of blood is no remission. It was therefore necessary that the patterns of things in the heavens should be purified with these; but the heavenly things themselves with better sacrifices than these. For Christ is not entered into the holy places made with hands, which are the figures of the true; but into heaven itself, now to appear in the presence of God for us: nor yet that he should offer himself often, as the high priest entereth into the holy place every year with blood of others; for then must he often have suffered since the foundation of the world: but now once in the end of the world hath he appeared to put away sin by the sacrifice of himself.*

Hebrews 9:22-26

When man sinned, God had to go as far as Heaven to correct it all because sin touches everything everywhere. In the earthly Holy of Holies given in Moses' time, before anyone could enter that sanctuary, an animal had to be sacrificed. Without that sacrifice,

God could not bring Heaven to Earth. Since man sinned, even the heavenly Holy of Holies was polluted. Just as the blood of animals was used to cleanse the earthly Holy of Holies, the blood of Jesus Christ was used to clean the heavenly Holy of Holies. God invested that much in man when He placed him in the Garden.

The great psalmist David said:

> *What is man, that thou art mindful of him? and the son of man, that thou visitest him?* Psalm 8:4

When David got the revelation of who man was, it was information to make one fearful. Man was destined for death and during what was called "life" here, he would live like a slave in the land. That was not what God intended.

Another meaning for Elohim, one of the names of God, is "Creator." The dominion of man went as far as the planets, including Satan himself. If God was the Creator, then man was in charge, for He put all things under our feet. That includes cancer. That includes poverty. That includes depression.

As believers in Christ, we are waging a war. I recently told Satan, "We're after you now! Enough is enough!" And you should do the same. Enough of every activity of Satan in your life! All you need to do is learn what Heaven is saying and say the same thing. God has put all things under our feet, and we know that the gifts and calling of God are without repentance:

> *For the gifts and calling of God are without repentance.*     Romans 11:29

What God gave Adam in creation can be yours today. Yes, you can experience *Heaven on Earth* right here and right now.

# CHAPTER 3

# WHAT DID JESUS DO TO BRING ABOUT HEAVEN ON EARTH?

*No man hath seen God at any time; the only begotten Son, which is in the bosom of the Father, he hath declared him.*

John 1:18

The Fall of man did not change the love of God for man, and it also did not change God's plan for man. God just had to find another man to carry out His plan so that mankind could get back what had been lost.

God had a plan, but Adam, the first man He put in charge, had "messed things up." Therefore, He had to get another man to stand in the place of Adam, to do the will of the Father.

When Jesus was being baptized, Father God testified of Him:

> *And Jesus, when he was baptized, went up straightway out of the water: and, lo, the heavens were opened unto him, and he saw the Spirit of God descending like a dove, and lighting upon him: and lo a voice from heaven, saying, This is my beloved Son, in whom I am well pleased.*　　　Matthew 3:16-17

God could not look to the fallen race of the Earth to bring forth the man He needed to bring redemption because everything on Earth had been polluted, and Satan was exercising the dominion man had ceded to him. Therefore, anything God would take from this Earth would already have been polluted.

If another Adam came from the Earth, Satan would still claim him. This was why, when God could not find anyone who didn't have the fallen nature of man and of the devil, He had to turn to Himself.

God turned to Himself to find a Son who had not known sin, who had not partaken of the sins of mankind, who did not have upon Himself the curse of spiritual death. Death must not have dominion over the man who would be called upon to redeem mankind.

What had once been in the Garden was the Kingdom of God on Earth. Eden was Heaven's headquarters here. All the information on how to rule this planet and its surrounding heavenly bodies was to be found in that place. Now Jesus' assignment was to restore Eden back to mankind, to establish the continuity of what God intended Eden to be in the first place.

Adam had lost it all when he died spiritually (before he died physically). Now, God decided that He would bring forth another Adam to be the firstborn. The original firstborn, Adam, "messed up" God's plan. Jesus would become the second Adam.

*The first man is of the earth, earthy; the second man is the Lord from heaven.*

1 Corinthians 15:47

The first thing this second Adam must do was to destroy the incumbent king, Satan himself. If He could not destroy the devil, the incumbent king, there was no way He could become the last Adam and redeem mankind from the Fall.

In order to accomplish this, the last Adam had to partake of the sin of man and then face the devil in combat. If He was able to win over him, fine. If He could not win this battle, then everything would become Satan's forever. The stakes were that high.

Most religious people think that Jesus died and then rose from the dead because it had already been programmed, but that's not so. This was a battle to the finish, and it was fought on equal terms. Jesus' chances were 50/50, and He was concerned (see Hebrews 5:6-7). That is why the Father sent angels to minister to His Son. If what He had set out to do had been an easy task, why would Jesus have prayed and asked the Father to take the cup from Him (see Matthew 26)?

This was a real battle. Jesus must not only taste of sin, He must become sin for us:

> *For he hath made him to be sin for us, who knew no sin; that we might be made the righteousness of God in him.*
> 2 Corinthians 5:21

Because He was made sin, Jesus must die, and then He must descend to Hell. Why? Because the Scriptures declare:

> *The soul that sinneth, it shall die.*
> Ezekiel 18:4 and 20

Yes, Jesus became sin, died, and went into the ravages of Hell for us. He did not have a sin nature, so it was up to the Father to place the sin of the whole world upon Him, just as if He (Jesus) were the one who had sinned.

Jesus must carry our sin and defeat the devil, otherwise He could not fulfill His assignment. That assignment was to free every man, woman, boy, and girl on this Earth from the dominion of Satan. To be the new Adam who would redeem mankind from the curse.

The coming of this Adam was not to be through a conception, like the first Adam. This was a conception by faith:

> *As many as received him to them gave he power to become the sons of God.*
>
> John 1:12

This conception was not between a man and a woman. It was a conception of faith between man and God Himself:

> *Which were born, not of blood, nor of the will of the flesh, nor of the will of man, but of God.*　　　John 1:13

Before Jesus did this, He had to destroy the one who was inputting sin into every human being. That is why He went to the cross and died.

Satan was delighted, thinking he had gained another victory, but he is the most foolish being on the Earth for allowing Jesus to go to the cross. By killing Jesus, Satan believed that he would win the battle of the ages. To the contrary, killing Jesus meant the devastation of Satan's kingdom:

> *Forasmuch then as the children are partakers of flesh and blood, he also himself likewise took part of the same; that through death he might destroy him that had the power of death, that is, the devil.* Hebrews 2:14

The resurrection of Jesus was a celebration for all humanity. Some religious leaders tell us not to eat meat at Easter, not even to put on shoes. If there was anytime we should eat everything, it is at Easter. If there is anytime we should wear the best clothes and shoes, it is Easter. This is the season to embarrass the devil.

Satan was totally defeated when Jesus rose from the dead, and that was the birth of the new Adam. This new Adam did not come by a conception through the union of a man and a woman, but by faith. The moment you receive Jesus into your life you, too, are born as a new Adam.

> *Therefore if any man be in Christ, he is a new creature: old things are passed away; behold, all things are become new.* 2 Corinthians 5:17

The new Adam was born of the Spirit:

> *Jesus answered and said unto him, Verily, verily, I say unto thee, Except a man be born again, he cannot see the kingdom of God.*
> *Nicodemus saith unto him, How can a man be born when he is old? can he enter the second time into his mother's womb, and be born?*
> *Jesus answered, Verily, verily, I say unto thee, Except a man be born of water and of the Spirit, he cannot enter into the kingdom of God. That which is born of the flesh is flesh; and that which is born of the Spirit is spirit.* John 3:3-6

This new man Adam was born again and born of the Spirit on his way to Eden. And you, too, can live in a modern Eden. Yes, you can experience *Heaven on Earth* right here and right now.

# CHAPTER 4

# WHAT IS THE NEW EDEN?

*According as his divine power hath given unto us all things that pertain unto life and godliness, through the knowledge of him that hath called us to glory and virtue: whereby are given unto us exceeding great and precious promises: that by these ye might be partakers of the divine nature, having escaped the corruption that is in the world through lust.* 2 Peter 1:3-4

Eden is no more physical, just as your new birth is not physical. The first Eden was a physical place where Adam and Eve lived and had everything they needed physically present for them, but the second Eden is not physical at all. This new Eden is in Christ, and all things are in Him—peace, satisfaction, provision, etc. That is why the apostle Paul could declare:

> *I can do all things through Christ which strengtheneth me.*    Philippians 4:13

There is no failure in the new Eden, and this Eden is the privilege of all who believe in Christ. As a believer, you are the most powerful being on the Earth because the assignment of Jesus was to raise up a new generation.

Jesus Himself became the firstborn of that generation and the example of how we should live. The moment you are born again, your nature changes, and you become "t*he righteousness of God*" in Christ:

> *Therefore if any man be in Christ, he is a new creature: old things are passed away; behold, all things are become new. And all things are of God, who hath reconciled us to himself by Jesus Christ,*

*and hath given to us the ministry of reconciliation; to wit, that God was in Christ, reconciling the world unto himself, not imputing their trespasses unto them; and hath committed unto us the word of reconciliation.*

*Now then we are ambassadors for Christ, as though God did beseech you by us: we pray you in Christ's stead, be ye reconciled to God. For he hath made him to be sin for us, who knew no sin; that we might be made the righteousness of God in him.* 2 Corinthians 5:17-21

*But ye are not in the flesh, but in the Spirit, if so be that the Spirit of God dwell in you. Now if any man have not the Spirit of Christ, he is none of his. And if Christ be in you, the body is dead because of sin; but the Spirit is life because of righteousness.*

Romans 8:9-10

Jesus' death and resurrection severed your ties to the first Adam, and now you are *"seated in heavenly places far above all principality and powers":*

> *The eyes of your understanding being enlightened; that ye may know what is the hope of his calling, and what the riches of the glory of his inheritance in the saints, and what is the exceeding greatness of his power to us-ward who believe, according to the working of his mighty power, which he wrought in Christ, when he raised him from the dead, and set him at his own right hand in the heavenly places, far above all principality, and power, and might, and dominion, and every name that is named, not only in this world, but also in that which is to come: and hath put all things under his feet, and gave him to be the head over all things to the church, which is his body, the fulness of him that filleth all in all.* Ephesians 1:18-23

Your position and your dominion over the Earth is unquestionable because Jesus

Christ, who is the Head of the new Creation, is no more seated in Heaven. He now lives inside of every believer, and He has promised:

> *Lo, I am with you always, even unto the end of the world.*    Matthew 28:20

So, if you are telling everyone that you are alone, you are mistaken. Jesus Himself is with you.

In this new creation, you are different from Adam—completely different. Whatever dominated Adam must not come near you at all because there is Somebody inside of you who is manifesting Heaven through you.

The first Adam gave birth to Cain, Abel, and Seth. The last Adam gave birth to the Church. If you are part of the Church, you don't have any business with the sin of Adam.

> *For whatsoever is born of God overco-meth the world: and this is the victory*

> *that overcometh the world, even our faith. Who is he that overcometh the world, but he that believeth that Jesus is the Son of God?*     1 John 5:4-5

Declare today, "I am an overcomer because of my new birth." Yes, you have been disconnected from Adam. The moment you became born again, every attribute of Jesus entered into you that very moment.

You cannot live like Jesus without everything Jesus has being in you by faith. This is not a physical experience; it is by faith. Everything in Christ is in you. His glory, power, and potency are in you by faith.

> *Herein is our love made perfect, that we may have boldness in the day of judgment: because as he is, so boldness in the day of judgment: because as he is, so are we in this world.*     1 John 4:17

You have every right to live like Jesus on the Earth, not because of your struggle or your intelligence, but because you are born of the Spirit (born again).

My children don't need to pay me a dime or beg me to look like me. All of them look like me, talk like me, and act like me. Why? Because they are mine. There is a gene inside me that is in them too.

It is the same when you are born again; the gene of God is in you. You may not have noticed it because you have been deceived, and that is the assignment of the devil. Know that the devil's power has been taken from him, so he uses lies, deception, and misinformation to keep people under his control.

The moment you are not hearing from the King that redeemed you and, instead, you are getting information from the devil, he will control you, just like he did the first Adam.

When Adam got his information from the serpent, he soon fell. The moment you listen to Satan, instead of what the Lord is saying, he has you in his net.

If you have been born again, you are freed from Satan's power, reconnected to the Source of all life and empowered to rule and reign. Yes, you can experience *Heaven on Earth* right here and right now.

# WHAT DOES IT MEAN TO BE "LIKE JESUS"?

*But if the Spirit of him that raised up Jesus from the dead dwell in you, he that raised up Christ from the dead shall also quicken your mortal bodies by his Spirit that dwelleth in you.* Romans 8:1

The term *Christian* originally meant "little Christ" or "Christlike." We are like Jesus right now, not when we get to Heaven. And yet how many church people are aware of this and wake up every morning knowing that Jesus is the One who has woken up inside of them? How many people declare their dominion over sickness, poverty, and oppression daily? How many people look at the storms of life and calmly say to them, "Peace, be still!"?

Very few people are doing this. The majority of those who are called Christians are weeping in despair. The enemy wants to bring everyone down to his level, back to where we used to be. He wants to make sure that everyone is still a victim under his dominion, and he uses his falsehoods to put people into bondage and keep them there.

It is very difficult for Satan to gain the trust of the new creations, except when they agree with him against the Word of God. Often, what Satan tells you is so logical (in fact, he will prove it with a lot of facts). Facts come through your mind, but truth comes through your spirit. Too often, what people call "reality" comes through their flesh. If you cannot discern and you agree with facts through your mind, you knock God out of the picture.

The Bible says you *have tasted the power of the world to come"*:

*For it is impossible for those who were once enlightened, and have tasted of the heavenly gift, and were made partakers of the Holy Ghost, and have tasted the good word of God, and the powers of the world to come, if they shall fall away, to renew them again unto repentance; seeing they crucify to themselves the Son of God afresh, and put him to an open shame.* Hebrews 6:4-6

Satan should no longer be an issue for us. Jesus has risen from the dead, and Satan knows he cannot put his hand on you when you know your rights as a believer in Christ. Just let the enemy know that God is living in you. I don't say this because I am a bishop, but because I am redeemed. This is the secret of my daily victory.

When you are saved, there is a re-connection with Heaven. When you are redeemed, there is inseparable connection made between you and Jesus, the Head of the Church. The Bible says that He is *"the true vine"* and you are *"the branches"*:

*I am the true vine, and my Father is the husbandman. Every branch in me that beareth not fruit he taketh away: and every branch that beareth fruit, he purgeth it, that it may bring forth more fruit.*

*Now ye are clean through the word which I have spoken unto you. Abide in me, and I in you. As the branch cannot bear fruit of itself, except it abide in the vine; no more can ye, except ye abide in me. I am the vine, ye are the branches: He that abideth in me, and I in him, the same bringeth forth much fruit: for without me ye can do nothing.*          John 15:1-5

Everything that is in the Vine is in you too, for you are connected to the vine. Therefore, everything in the vine comes to you on a daily basis.

You have been given a body just as a cover for your spirit. It is your responsibility to take care of that body. If you lose your body, you stop touching the physical, but your spirit lives on. Your spirit cannot die, but the flesh can:

*The spirit of a man will sustain his infirmity; but a wounded spirit who can bear?*                Proverbs 18:14

When your body dies, it is because you refuse or are no longer able to carry it along with the spirit. Nobody can be sick when their spirit is healthy. The spirit of a man will sustain his body. So, the stronger your spirit, the stronger your body will be.

If your spirit is lean, it is not feeding on the truth, and all you know is religion, when pressure comes, you will not be able to stand. Even when you say no to temptation, you must be able to explain why you are saying no. You must declare, "It is written, 'By His stripes I am healed.' Therefore, Satan, get thee behind me." When you have proof or evidence, and the enemy doesn't have any evidence, he will leave you alone.

Yes, the stronger your spirit, the stronger your body. Don't let the devil take your body before your assignment on Earth is finished. You are only permitted to die when your assignment is complete.

There is nothing quite like a sudden death in the Body of Christ. The patriarchs had meetings with their family members before they left the Earth, and they were not even washed with the blood of Christ. Paul, the apostle, was negotiating with death. He said:

> *According to my earnest expectation and my hope, that in nothing I shall be ashamed, but that with all boldness, as always, so now also Christ shall be magnified in my body, whether it be by life, or by death. For to me to live is Christ, and to die is gain. But if I live in the flesh, this is the fruit of my labour: yet what I shall choose I wot not. For I am in a strait betwixt two, having a desire to depart, and to be with Christ; which is far better: nevertheless to abide in the flesh is more needful for you.*
>
> Philippians 1:20-24

For the sake of the people he ministered to, he decided to stay, and the same precious blood that washed Paul has washed you and me too.

The spirit of a man will sustain his infirmities. Therefore, declare to yourself, "I am sustained." You are the carrier of life with the Spirit of God on the inside of you. You carry the anointing within:

No matter how weak your body may feel today, I declare that you are healed. The Spirit brings life to every dead part of your body. Stop listening to things that are intellectually and spiritually defective.

The sin issue the devil is tormenting you about is no longer there. It was laid on the body of Jesus, and two people cannot be punished for the same offence. It's illegal, so stop suffering because of it.

My Bible tells me that it is through one man's offence (that of Adam) that we received death, and is it through one man's obedience (that of Jesus) that we have regained life:

*For if by one man's offence death reigned by one; much more they which receive*

> *abundance of grace and of the gift of righteousness shall reign in life by one, Jesus Christ.*　　　　Romans 5:17

Therefore, declare to yourself, "I have life!" Then believe it and act on it.

Life was lost in the Garden of Eden, but life is regained through Christ. The new Eden must continue. Therefore, you must be healed, you must be financially blessed, your must be anointed, you must be perfected in the mighty name of Jesus.

You have been given the earnest of the Spirit to continue on the Earth, just as Jesus was:

> *For all the promises of God in him are yea, and in him Amen, unto the glory of God by us. Now he which stablisheth us with you in Christ, and hath anointed us, is God; who hath also sealed us, and given the earnest of the Spirit in our hearts.*　　　　2 Corinthians 1:20-22

During Jesus' first thirty years here on Earth, He didn't perform any miracles. Then the Holy Ghost came upon Him, and when the Holy Ghost came upon Him, the story changed. He was now operating at the level of divinity.

Before Jesus left the Earth, He told everyone that it was expedient for Him to go, but that He was sending the Holy Spirit to *"abide with you forever"*:

> *And I will pray the Father, and he shall give you another Comforter, that he may abide with you forever.* John 14:16

Could Jesus have lied? Certainly not. Declare this, "I have the same Holy Spirit, and He is abiding in me right now." This should assure you of the ability of living in a heavenly realm here. Yes, you can experience *Heaven on Earth* right here and right now.

CHAPTER 6

# WHAT DOES IT MEAN TO LIVE IN THE LIGHT AND TO SPEAK LIGHT?

*And God said, Let there be light: and there was light.* Genesis 1:3

In Genesis 1, the Bible describes the Earth as being dark and chaotic. Then the Spirit moved upon the waters, and God the Father declared, *"Let there be light!"* When He said that, everything changed. Suddenly, *"there was light!"*

No matter how things are with you right now, I want you to know you that have the same Spirit in you that was in Jesus. You were created to live in the light. Therefore, you must be able to declare what God has said about you. It is when you speak it that the Spirit of God brings it to pass.

It is not you that will cause the effect. As a new creature, the Spirit is in you when you speak, and the Spirit of God will bring the results. Jesus said:

> *For verily I say unto you, That whoso-*
> *ever shall say unto this mountain, Be*
> *thou removed, and be thou cast into the*
> *sea; and shall not doubt in his heart, but*
> *shall believe that those things which he*
> *saith shall come to pass; he shall have*
> *whatsoever he saith. Therefore I say*
> *unto you, What things soever ye desire,*
> *when ye pray, believe that ye receive*
> *them, and ye shall have them.*
>
> Mark 11:23-24

Your ability was not mentioned here. Your responsibility is to speak, and it is the Spirit of God that springs into action. In this way, you can remove mountains and stand your ground against any enemy. You have so much authority on this planet that you can control anything.

Joshua, a man under the Old Covenant, was fighting with the Ammonites late one day when night began to fall:

> *Then spake Joshua to the* LORD *in the day when the* LORD *delivered up the Amorites before the children of Israel, and he said in the sight of Israel, Sun, stand thou still upon Gibeon; and thou, Moon, in the valley of Ajalon. And the sun stood still, and the moon stayed, until the people had avenged themselves upon their enemies. Is not this written in the book of Jasher? So the sun stood still in the midst of heaven, and hasted not to go down about a whole day. And there was no day like that before it or after it, that the* LORD *hearkened unto the voice of a man: for the* LORD *fought for Israel.*                Joshua 10:12-14

Joshua did not have the name of Jesus, no advocate, no intercessor, and yet he boldly spoke to the sun, "Stay where you are until I finish this battle with the Amorites!" And God heard what His servant had said. This is the power God has given us, as His representatives on Earth.

When the Spirit moved at Creation, God spoke. His declaration caused the ugliness to recede, and the beauty of creation to come forth. And the same Spirit that brought it all about is in you right now.

You have the Spirit of God in you, and therefore you are able to declare a thing and see it come to pass. When you speak, the Spirit of God in you will bring the result. Why? Because you are a child of the Living God.

Joshua, a man, spoke, and the sun and moon obeyed him. When you speak, your blood and your bones must listen, your finances must listen, and principalities and powers must listen, because the Spirit of the Living God is upon you too.

The new Adam and new Eve are different from the Adam and Eve in Eden. This Adam and Eve are living in Christ.

Thank God for a man who spoke to the sun and those who spoke to the heavens, but the Bible is clear: God has provided better things for you and me.

> *God having provided some better thing for us, that they without us should not be made perfect.* Hebrews 11:40

It's time to live in Heaven here on Earth. Although we are in this world, Jesus said that we are not *"of the world"*:

> *If ye were of the world, the world would love his own: but because ye are not of the world, but I have chosen you out of the world, therefore the world hateth you.* John 15:19

Jesus showed us that there is a heavenly system that can operate here on Earth by faith. He did not die on the cross just so that we could go to Heaven; He died so that we could live here on Earth in dominion over the devil. He died to bring Heaven back to Earth.

I love to humiliate the devil, and I have been doing it now for more than thirty years. Some years ago, I was doing a seminar with the theme "Long Life," and I went into the Word to dig out why believers must not die young. After the first night, I had a vision in which I saw some believers I knew. They were telling me that if they had known all these things, they would not have died. "Well," I told them, "you have already died, so there is nothing we can do about it now."

On the second day, I saw a group of people waiting to kill me. I told them, "If you don't leave me, I will kill you," and they left me.

On the fourth day, Death himself came with something in his hand and wanted to hit me on the head. I said, "You can never!" When I said that, Death vanished, and I woke up. Death is a toy in the hands of a believer.

The Bible says:

*O death, where is thy sting? O grave, where is thy victory?*

1 Corinthians 15:55

Jesus Christ has given us victory over death. The devil may tell you that you are going to die, but it's a lie. Anything that is not in the Word of God is a lie. Why should you see a casket in your dream and then not be able to sleep? Maybe the casket makers decided to advertise in your dreams. That doesn't make it real. Death is not what the Bible declares over your life. Instead, it declares:

*With long life will I satisfy him, and shew him my salvation.* Psalm 91:16

God didn't say, "I will show you caskets." If you see a casket in your dream, wake up and send that casket back to the owner. Can you imagine Death threatening the casket owner?

Can you imagine Death threatening Jesus? I cannot imagine it. In fact, the Bible says that He died *"by the determinate counsel and foreknowledge of God"*:

*Him, being delivered by the determinate counsel and foreknowledge of God, ye*

**65**

> *have taken, and by wicked hands have*
> *crucified and slain.* Acts 2:23

Jesus Himself said:

> *As the Father knoweth me, even so know*
> *I the Father: and I lay down my life for*
> *the sheep. ... Therefore doth my Father*
> *love me, because I lay down my life, that*
> *I might take it again. No man taketh it*
> *from me, but I lay it down of myself. I*
> *have power to lay it down, and I have*
> *power to take it again. This command-*
> *ment have I received of my Father.*
> John 10:15 and 17-18

You and I need to come to the point that the devil is no longer dictating to us. We should be dictating to him because Christ is alive forevermore, and He lives in us.

The new Adam and Eve have been born, and we are no longer connected with the first Adam at all. So, stop saying, "If not for the sin of Adam, we wouldn't be in this situation." God knows that if you had been there in Eden, you probably would have eaten every fruit from that tree.

In fact, you are still partaking of the forbidden fruit. What do I mean by that? Anytime God says to you, "You are rich," and you reply, "No, I'm not," you have just eaten the tree of the tree of poverty. When God says, "You are healed," and you say, "I'm still sick," you have just eaten the fruit of the tree of sickness. It's time for your victory, and that victory is possible because the Son of God is alive in you. I want you to take that victory today and to take it every day from this time forward. Start speaking life and light, and things will change for you. Yes, you can experience *Heaven on Earth* right here and right now.

# CHAPTER 7

# WHY IS IT NECESSARY TO GIVE VOICE TO YOUR PROMISES?

*Death and life are in the power of the tongue: and they that love it shall eat the fruit thereof.* Proverbs 18:21

The Spirit of God is upon you, but He won't act until you open your mouth and declare what God has promised. Jesus Christ has anointed you, but that anointing will not gain expression until you open your mouth and speak forth His truths.

Right now, wherever you are, open your mouth and declare, "I am born of the Spirit. Therefore, every opposition to my rulership must bow in the name of Jesus. I am a king in Christ. I am anointed, and Jesus Christ lives in me. Therefore, anything standing against my rulership must go now in the name of Jesus Christ. Financially, materially, and spiritually ... anything limiting me I command to bow." Yes, you have that power.

God brought all the animals to Adam, and he gave them names, and God says to you today, "You need to begin naming things. You need to say, 'I am blessed, I am anointed,' and 'I am prosperous.'"

In the life of Jesus, while He was still here on Earth, He named things. He said, "I am the way," "I am the truth," "I am the bread of life." He overcame through the words of His mouth.

Religion dictates that you must struggle for your blessings. Jesus is saying, "Just speak! Just declare it! Just give voice to your promises! I have given you that power."

What should you declare today? For example, "Everything that is meant for my joy, begin to manifest in Jesus' name." Yes, let today mark the end of all your struggles.

I respect professionals, but they don't have the final say over your life. How many of you know the Engineer who is charging the bulb the sun uses or the Engineer who designed the pillars that are holding up the Universe?

Scientists tell us that you breathe out carbon dioxide and breath in oxygen. The truth goes far beyond that. The Bible says that God breathed into man the breath of life, and man became a living soul (see Genesis 2:7).

I was just coming into this revelation, when they brought to me a two-year-old who had polio. I looked at him, held those feeble legs in my hands, and smiled. Then I breathed the life of God that is in me into that child, and the following day the boy began to run. Anything that cripples your destiny is destroyed right now in Jesus' name. Believe it.

It's awesome to be a part of God's Kingdom, to share from the Constitution of the Federal Republic of Heaven, and to know what is ours through that Constitution. This can enable us to live life without pain or stress. This is our promise of abundance in every part of our lives.

It is not enough to attend church. When you go, you must go with a hunger to learn. The purpose of going to church is not just to register your presence; it is to let the church be your school. If you go to church, but you are not passing the exams of life, something's wrong.

When you go to school, the teacher usually announces when a test will be coming and gives you time to prepare for it. In life, there is no announcement for the tests to come. They might come at any moment, and they often do. Every second is a test of life.

In our world today, there are so many things around you trying to disprove all that God has said. If you are not prepared, you might make a mess of the journey of life. You might let the lies of man rob you.

The decision is yours. Will you believe the lies of the evil one or will you believe the truths of God's Word? And if you believe the truths of God's Word, will you give voice to His promises, claiming what is rightfully yours? Will you continue to struggle in life, or will you accept God's invitation to leave this old world behind and become an active member of His Kingdom? Then His Blessings will flow freely in your everyday life. Yes, you can experience *Heaven on Earth* right here and right now.

# CHAPTER 8

# WHAT DOES IT MEAN TO EXPERIENCE TRUE PEACE?

*Therefore being justified by faith we have peace with God through our Lord Jesus Christ.* Roman 5:1

Peace is not just a state of mind, as the dictionary indicates. We misuse words when we don't know the foundation of them or the intent of the speaker. So many words have been turned into slang expressions that no longer convey their original meaning.

There are words in the Bible we can't use much now because the people of the world have changed their meaning. When you say, for example, that Jesus rode an ass into Jerusalem, people say, "What are you talking about?" At the mention of that word, they have something very different in mind, all because the world has perverted the meaning of a perfectly good scriptural word.

When children are making too much noise, many parents say, "Can I please have some peace around here?" We have come to think of peace as mere quietness, but that is another misuse of the word. Peace is a supernatural force that puts you in position to control every situation of your life.

I discovered in the Bible that the word *peace* is from the Greek word *shalom,* meaning "wholeness, completeness, prosperity, joy, peace, nothing missing and nothing broken." That is the real meaning of peace, and that changes everything, doesn't it?

You and I are supernatural people living in a natural world. We have come here to experience what the natural world is like. Many believe we are just natural people trying to experience the supernatural, but that's not the case. Somebody has been deceived. The devil came to steal, to kill, and to destroy, and he has succeeded in stealing many people's hearts and replacing them with his lies.

The great majority of believers don't really know who they are and are struggling in the world instead of dominating it and controlling it. You are not a natural person; you are a supernatural person who has been deceived into living a natural life.

What did Jesus say about it?

*Jesus answered and said unto him, verily, verily I say unto thee, except a man be born again he cannot see the kingdom of God.* John 3:3

This *born* does not refer to being conceived and given birth to by your parents. That is the first birth, and it doesn't guarantee you a supernatural life. Fools are born, just as wise men are born. What makes a difference in life is being born *"from above."*

> *And he said unto them, Ye are from beneath; I am from above: ye are of this world; I am not of this world.*
>
> John 8:23

Through Christ, we, too, can experience birth *"from above,"* and without it, we can never experience the Kingdom of God. Once we are born again, born of God, we are then a child of God, and our experiences should change. Since we are *"from above,"* we now have the right to experience Heaven on Earth.

What must you do to begin having this experience? You don't need to *do* anything; Jesus already did it all. You just need to believe in what He has already done on your behalf, and start living it here and now.

Living a victorious life is not as difficult as many think:

> *He that cometh from above is above all, he that is of the earth is earthly and speaketh of the earth, he that cometh from heaven is above all.* John 3:31

The things of Earth are not to govern your life. Sickness, disease, poverty, and affliction are not to rule over you. You are above them all, and you therefore have the peace of God. Nothing is to be broken or missing in your life. As we have seen, Paul wrote:

> *Therefore being justified by faith we have peace with God through our Lord Jesus Christ.*                Roman 5:1

Many times, when Christians hear the Word of God preached, they are inspired to joy and rejoicing. Few, however, go on to meditate more deeply on the Word. As a result, faith is not born in their hearts, and boldness does not become part of their nature. They hear, but they fail to go deeper. We must meditate on the Word until it is converted into power for practical living.

Tradition and religion have taught us things that God never said. For instance, that Jesus Christ died for us, He rose from the dead, and He is alive forevermore. In that process, He took power from the devil and paid the full price for our forgiveness and healing so that the devil would leave us alone. Something about that doesn't sound right to me. Why would you pay someone you never owed anything to?

What did we possibly owe the devil? He has caused us noting but affliction, disease, and death. The only reason he had any access to our lives is that were separated from God. Jesus died to remedy that.

One day two of my children were making a lot of noise in our home, quarrelling and shouting at one another, until I finally told them, "If I hear your voice one more time today, you're going to be in big trouble." But as soon as I was out of sight, they started up again.

This time I told them, "I wanted to take you out to buy some of the things you needed, but you can forget about it now." They looked at each other and said, "Are we really fighting?" Then they hugged and made up and came and told me they were finished and we could go to the store.

Why do I tell that story? What God is saying to us is this: "Satan has access to your life only because there was a misunderstanding between us. When you fail to walk in My precepts, you are a sinner, and are standing against My will. But Someone came to reconcile you back to Me. His name is Jesus, and through Him, you have been not only been reconciled back to Me, but the fight is over." It is finished, Satan. You have no right to continue to afflict God's people.

Being justified by faith, we have peace with God. If you don't know that, the devil will trouble you constantly and tell you it's all "because of your past." Just tell the devil, "I don't have a past, and if I did have a past, it would be no concern of yours."

I have discovered this kind of peace with God, and let me tell you this: it cannot be found anywhere except in Jesus. If you search for peace outside of Jesus, you will end up in pieces.

Jesus Himself said:

*Peace I leave with you, my peace I give unto you: not as the world giveth, give I unto you. Let not your heart be troubled, neither let it be afraid.*

John 14:27

God is not expecting you to use your own peace. He is offering you His peace, His *shalom.*

Many years ago, the Holy Spirit said to me, "Anytime you are worried or troubled, check what you are believing, and you will find that it is not from Me." It's true. Each time fear grips your heart, you are telling God, "Jesus is not enough for me."

All your weeping won't change anything. There are two things that will make all the different in your life: (1) What you know, and (2) What you believe. You must know that you are loved by God:

*Herein is love that he loved us that he sent his son to be propitiation for our sin.*
1 John 4:10

This is why, no matter how terrible your case may be, God can never be angry with you. If He is not answering your prayer, it is not because He is angry with you or has abandoned you. It is because of your lack of faith in what He has promised. We serve a God who even allows rain to fall on the vineyard of a wicked person. Even a wicked person still gets sunshine, and both rain and sunshine are supplied by Almighty God. How much more will He hear and answer the prayers of His beloved children! Yes, you can experience *Heaven on Earth* right here and right now.

CHAPTER 9

# WHY IS IT SO IMPORTANT TO UNDERSTAND THE LOVE OF GOD?

*The grace of the Lord Jesus Christ, and the love of God, and the communion of the Holy Ghost, be with you all. Amen.*
2 Corinthians 13:14

We are talking about a loving Father, and if you are not sure of His love for you, you will question everything. In fact, you will live in guilt. You will live in fear. You will live in shame, and something will keep telling you that you are not getting the best in life because of what you have done or because you have not been able to do enough.

But what is the true measure of *enough*? Could our own efforts ever be enough?

God is saying to you today, "If you will understand that I love you with all My passion, you will discover that My love fully covers a multitude of sins." He has said in His Word:

> *Hatred stirreth up strifes: but love covereth all sins.* Proverbs 10:12

> *And above all things have fervent charity among yourselves: for charity shall cover the multitude of sins.* 1 Peter 4:8

When you know that you are loved by God, instead of continuing to sin, you will be restrained from sinning. You must know and understand that the covenant that God made with Jesus covers everything that concerns you, everything that pertains to your *"life and godliness"*:

> *According as his divine power hath given unto us all things that pertain unto*

*life and godliness, through the knowl-*
*edge of him that hath called us to glory*
*and virtue: whereby are given unto us*
*exceeding great and precious promises:*
*that by these ye might be partakers of*
*the divine nature, having escaped the*
*corruption that is in the world through*
*lust.*                                    2 Peter 1:3-4

This came about because of an agreement between God and His Son, Jesus. You came in into the picture because of faith, but He had already perfected everything and settled everything when He rose from the dead.

As He was hanging on the cross for your sins, Jesus cried out:

*It is finished.*                         John 19:30

What did He mean by that? He meant, "I have made a new beginning for these people." That's why the Scriptures tell us:

*But as many as received him, to them*
*gave he power to become the sons of God,*

**87**

> *even to them that believe on his name:*
> *which were born, not of blood, nor of the*
> *will of the flesh, nor of the will of man,*
> *but of God.* John 1:12-13

How proud would you be if you were a child of the President of the United States. I have never seen a son or daughter of any president of any country who was on welfare. No, everything is completely taken care of for them, and they don't need to think about anything. You and I are the sons and daughters of the most high God. If things are not working for you, then you don't know your Heavenly Dad very well. The moment you know Him, that changes everything. You need to have this understanding.

Far too many of God's children struggle with the situations of life, when His Word tells us to stop struggling and enter into His rest:

> *For we which have believed do enter into*
> *rest, as he said, As I have sworn in my*
> *wrath, if they shall enter into my rest:*

*although the works were finished from the foundation of the world.*

Hebrews 4:3

We were not meant to struggle like other people. Why should we struggle? We are the King's kids. When you know this truth, not just in theory, but in daily practice, your life will change. You will rest in the assurance of God's love for you, and His blessings will flow to you as never before. Yes, you can experience *Heaven on Earth* right here and right now.

# CHAPTER 10

# WHY IS IT SO IMPORTANT TO BELIEVE WHAT GOD SAYS?

*God is not a man, that he should lie; neither the son of man, that he should repent: hath he said, and shall he not do it? or hath he spoken, and shall he not make it good?*  Numbers 23:19

When God speaks, He expects what He has said to be fulfilled. Therefore, when He speaks, He seeks for those who will believe what He says. That Word travels from house to house, seeking a believer, irrespective of age, color, or location because that Word must not *"return void"*:

> *So shall my word be that goeth forth out*
> *of my mouth: it shall not return unto me*
> *void, but it shall accomplish that which*
> *I please, and it shall prosper in the thing*
> *whereto I sent it.*　　　Isaiah 55:11

When God releases a word of prosperity, a word of healing, a word of progress, a word of breakthrough, that word must not return void. It must accomplish something in someone's life. That word was designed to bring results. The results, however, depend on that word finding a believing heart. Someone must take hold of that word, believe it, and act on it.

When Mary, the mother of Jesus, visited her cousin Elizabeth, Elizabeth prophesied to her:

> *And blessed is she that believed, for*
> *there shall be a performance of those*
> *things which were told her from the*
> *Lord.*　　　　　Luke 1:45

When you believe, there is a performance of what you have believed.

Therefore, it is not God's fault if things are not happening in your life. His Word is designed for performance, for fulfillment, for action, but if it does not find a believing heart, one that agrees with what He is saying, what can God do?

God is a God of results, a God of performance, a God of actions. Therefore it is wisdom on your part to take hold of any word He has spoken. What do you have to lose? You know that it cannot return void, it cannot fail to bear fruit, it cannot fail to bring results. If you believe it, God will do it.

God the Father sent Jesus into this world to bring peace on earth through a new order of government. Isaiah foretold:

> *For unto us a child is born, unto us a son is given: and the government shall be upon his shoulder: and his name shall be called Wonderful, Counsellor, The mighty God, The everlasting Father, The Prince of Peace. Of the increase of*

> *his government and peace there shall be*
> *no end, upon the throne of David, and*
> *upon his kingdom, to order it, and to*
> *establish it with judgment and with jus-*
> *tice from henceforth even for ever. The*
> *zeal of the* LORD *of hosts will perform*
> *this.* Isaiah 9:6-7

Through Jesus, God set up a Kingdom on this Earth that was brought about to eradicate the government of Satan and all man-made systems, and the focus of this Kingdom is to bring peace.

When we are born again, we become part of that Kingdom:

> *Who hath delivered us from the power*
> *of darkness and hath translated us into*
> *the kingdom of his dear son. In whom*
> *we have redemption through his blood,*
> *even the forgiveness of sins: who is the*
> *image of the invisible God, the firstborn*
> *of every creature: for by him were all*
> *things created, that are in heaven, and*
> *that are in earth, visible and invisible,*

*whether they be thrones, or dominions, or principalities, or powers: all things were created by him, and for him: and he is before all things, and by him all things consist.* Colossians 1:13-17

The King came with the government of peace, and He says that we have been translated into the Kingdom He created. We need to have this understanding. With God's *shalom*, everything is flowing, and nothing is missing. Yes, you can experience *Heaven on Earth* right here and right now.

# CHAPTER 11

# WHY IS IT IMPORTANT TO RECOGNIZE JESUS AS KING?

*Whatsoever the LORD pleased, that did he in heaven, and in earth, in the seas, and all deep places.* Psalm 135:6

We must have the understanding that God is a king and that He rules from an invisible realm called Heaven. From that invisible realm, He controls everything on the Earth. His throne in Heaven governs everything that happens in the natural.

The physical does not control the spiritual. In fact, the physical is just an offshoot of the spiritual. The spiritual is more real than the physical. The physical is just a picture or an image of the real.

From the realm of the Spirit, God can prevent or alter anything in the physical, and the physical cannot stop God from doing what He is doing. He does *"whatsoever [He] pleases."*

In other words, if something pleases God in Heaven, the Earth cannot stop Him from fulfilling His dream. And it pleases God that you live in sound health and prosperity and experience long life, and, therefore, that is what is coming to pass in your life right now in Jesus' name.

Because God is a king, not a president or a prime minister, He establishes His will through decrees. He will not dialogue with you. He is not a democrat or a republican , and He does not use the rules of democracy. He rules by decree because He knows better than any man or woman and understands exactly what you need.

You may not even know what you need, but God does:

> *Therefore I say unto you, Take no thought for your life, what ye shall eat,*

*or what ye shall drink; nor yet for your body, what ye shall put on. Is not the life more than meat, and the body than raiment? Behold the fowls of the air: for they sow not, neither do they reap, nor gather into barns; yet your heavenly Father feedeth them. Are ye not much better than they?*

*Which of you by taking thought can add one cubit unto his stature? And why take ye thought for raiment? Consider the lilies of the field, how they grow; they toil not, neither do they spin: and yet I say unto you, That even Solomon in all his glory was not arrayed like one of these.*

*Wherefore, if God so clothe the grass of the field, which to day is, and to morrow is cast into the oven, shall he not much more clothe you, O ye of little faith? Therefore take no thought, saying, What shall we eat? or, What shall we drink? or, Wherewithal shall we be clothed? (For after all these things do the Gentiles seek:) for your heavenly Father knoweth*

> *that ye have need of all these things. But*
> *seek ye first the kingdom of God, and his*
> *righteousness; and all these things shall*
> *be added unto you.* Matthew 6:25-33

The Father knows what we need even before we ask Him. Therefore, He can rule by decree, to establish His will. He knows what can happen to cause things to go wrong. He masterminded everything before anything came into existence, and He is able to do more than any of us even think or imagine:

> *Now unto him that is able to do exceed-*
> *ing abundantly above all that we ask*
> *or think, according to the power that*
> *worketh in us.* Ephesians 3:20

And God does it all because of His love for us. He knows what you need because He loves you so much. He not only knows what you need; He knows when you need it and the best way to supply it.

Because God is love, His decrees are always for our benefit. His will never hurts anyone; it brings us ever closer to our purpose for existence:

> *(For I know the thoughts that I think toward you, saith the* LORD, *thoughts of peace, and not of evil, to give you an expected end.)*      Jeremiah 29:11

In the Scriptures, we discover that because of God's mighty hands and His glorious power, He doesn't need anyone to counsel or advise Him:

> *Who hath directed the Spirit of the* LORD, *or being his counsellor hath taught him? With whom took he counsel, and who instructed him, and taught him in the path of judgment, and taught him knowledge, and shewed to him the way of understanding? Behold, the nations are as a drop of a bucket, and are counted as the small dust of the balance: behold, he taketh up the isles as a very little thing. And Lebanon is not sufficient to burn, nor*

> *the beasts thereof sufficient for a burnt*
> *offering.* Isaiah 40:13-16

Man trying to counsel God would be like a newborn trying to advise a university professor. It's not possible, right?

Because God's love is so strong, His plans are to give every citizen peace with no evil along their path, and the instrument He uses to establish this is His Word. God's Word is the expression or how He feels. It is the expression of His plans. Just as in the physical, we have laws that govern us, God's Word is the law of the Spirit.

If you doubt the physical laws, try jumping from a high place. The Law of Gravity will quickly take over. It is always present.

Why would you ever doubt the spiritual laws? You don't need to pray about it or seek a second opinion on it. You don't need to fast and pray about it. It's the law, and it works whether you know it or not. Just as the physical laws govern everything that we do in the physical, the laws of God govern everything we do in the Spirit. The key to those laws and their effect on your life is your faith.

Yes, our God is a king, He rules by His Word, and His Word is His law, His constitution. Every time He speaks, those words become law for us.

> *Where the word of a king is, there is power: and who may say unto him, What doest thou?*     Ecclesiastes 8:4

Who indeed? You can't bend God's will. You could never stand against Him. Therefore, His Word is law.

When God called Joshua to take over for Moses and lead the children of Israel back into the Promised Land, he told him exactly what to do to accomplish it:

> *This book of the law shall not depart out of thy mouth; but thou shalt meditate therein day and night, that thou mayest observe to do according to all that is written therein: for then thou shalt make*

**103**

> *thy way prosperous, and then thou shalt*
> *have good success.* Joshua 1:8

Joshua was not just a lucky person; he was blessed because he followed the law of his King. That made his success automatic. When you follow the law of the King, there is no demon from Hell that can stop you.

To stop the law of the King would be to stop God Himself, and who could do that? When you stand on His Word and obey what it says, it's as if you are putting God into action. It's like putting God to the test. When you obey the law of the King, God is not asking you to do anything else. Just release your faith, and the blessings will automatically flow to you. It cannot fail. Yes, you can experience *Heaven on Earth* right here and right now.

# CHAPTER 12

# WHY IS THE SEED SO IMPORTANT?

*And the LORD God planted a garden eastward in Eden; and there he put the man whom he had formed.*

Genesis 2:8

I find it to be interesting that when God created the Earth, He did it like a farmer, not like a technologist, an accountant, or even a medical doctor. The first thing God did was plant a garden.

Why did God do that? Because He wanted to establish a principle that would work for any person on Earth, no matter where they lived or what they did for a living. He said:

*While the earth remaineth, seedtime and
harvest, and cold and heat, and summer
and winter, and day and night shall not
cease.*                    Genesis 8:22

In this way, God put Himself under the
law that He had established. He was saying,
"I will initiate life on this planet as a farmer.
If you follow Me, no matter what profession
you belong to, you will get results. I will
rule this planet by the law of the Spirit that
manifests in the physical."

Based on this, how could any believer in
Christ confess that they are poor? Something
must be wrong with them. In the Body of
Christ, there should be no poverty whatsoever. You might ask, "What about those
people who seem to be so zealous for God
and yet are poor?" Well, they are clearly
missing something.

The Word of the Lord declares that He
gives seed to the sower:

*Now he that ministereth seed to the
sower both minister bread for your food,*

*and multiply your seed sown, and increase the fruits of your righteousness.*
2 Corinthians 9:10

Why does God do this? He does it because it is the only way this world's system (the Babylonian system) would not be able to rule over His children. He gives you seed. If you will plant that seed, you are then qualified for a harvest. If, for some reason, God did not allow that harvest to come, then we could question His integrity and the integrity of His Word. That will never happen. His harvests are sure.

If you are broke, what is going on? Check your obedience. Are you sowing the seed God provided for you as instructed by Him?

When we talk about seed in church, people get nervous, thinking that we about to launch a fund-raising. But, with God, inside or outside of the Church, seed is a serious business. God wants to prosper you, but He needs your cooperation.

When God blesses us, it is not just so that we can throw money around town. His

**107**

desire is always to further His Kingdom in the hearts of men. If you are in need, learn the principles of sowing and reaping.

Some people seem to be good sowers, and yet they also seem to lack an understanding of spiritual things. For instance, when it comes time for Holy Communion in the church, they take it like it was any snack. Some people pay their tithes and are still not blessed because they don't understand the ways of God.

Paying your tithes is not just some religious activity that you do every Sunday. "Oh, I'd better pay my tithe," some say, "or God will be running after me." Is that any reason to be paying your tithe? Do you not know that tithing is a key that will unlock the windows of Heaven over your life?

Everything that God says has a purpose behind it. Check your Bible. You were not destined to struggle or to be poor. If you have a seed in your hand, that seed is the key to your future.

Yes, your money is a seed. Think about it. A farmer trusts the earth enough to put his precious seed into the ground and cover it. Then, he goes home, fully expecting a harvest to come. If a farmer can trust the earth that much, why don't you put your seed into God's good earth and trust Him for a harvest?

Some people seem to enjoy struggling in life. No matter what you do for them, they are always in the same condition. "Well, I'm trying," they say. Who asked you to try? God only asked you to believe and obey.

It is right to pity the poor and struggling, but sometimes I cannot pity them. They seem to be married to their struggle.

"I have nothing," they declare. That's a lie. They have money for Coke when they get thirsty. What might they reap if they planted that Coca-Cola money? Instead of using their money to go somewhere, what if they planted it, investing it in God's Kingdom? God said:

*But this I say, He which soweth sparingly shall reap also sparingly; and he which soweth bountifully shall reap also bountifully.* 2 Corinthians 9:6

And God can't lie. This is not the word of the Bishop; it is the Word of the Lord. He went on to say:

> *Every man according as he purposeth in his heart, so let him give ; not grudgingly, or of necessity: for God loveth a cheerful giver. And God is able to make all grace abound toward you; that ye, always having all sufficiency in all things, may abound to every good work.*
>
> 2 Corinthians 9:7-8

So, spiritual sowing is giving. Release your faith by releasing that seed, and the reward will come.

You were not destined to be poor, and God put seed in your hands to see what you would do with it. Don't wait until you become a millionaire before you start practicing the law of seedtime and harvest. It is the sowing of what is in your hand that will bring you the answer you need.

The reason many believers are poor is not because there is no more money in God's economy; it is because many will not yield to the Spirit of God when He prompts them to give. You are a steward of your seed, but God is in charge of the harvest. So, don't be concerned about the harvest; be concerned that you do the right thing with your seed.

The system of the world is to work you as much as possible, pay you as little as possible, and keep you deeply indebted. God can take you out of that system if you will obey Him. If you stay in the world's system, that's where you will die.

God has a glorious future for you. It will come as you are faithful with your seed. Jesus taught:

> *His lord said unto him, Well done, thou good and faithful servant: thou hast been faithful over a few things, I will make thee ruler over many things: enter thou into the joy of thy lord.*
>
> Matthew 25:21

If you have not become a faithful sower, God cannot entrust more seed into your hands. If every time He puts seeds into your hands, you eat it, what can you expect?

You may think you have hit a jackpot, but you will soon be disappointed to find yourself licking the pot. If you will trust God and His Word, you can become a ruler on this Earth.

Some very nice people who love God with all their heart seem to be always burdened down with bills. They want to serve God, but their bills have said no, and, because of that, they have been reduced to serving this world.

The answer is not just another job. Some work two jobs and still can't make a go of it. Jobs can wear you out. In some families, both father and mother are working so many hours that they can no longer take their family to church, and still they can't get ahead.

This world's system was not designed for your benefit; it was designed to keep you under its control. All that can be said of some people at their funeral is that they were "good workers." "He gave twenty-five years of his life to the company he worked for." Well, that's good, but was he a slave because he couldn't do anything else? Did he have any choice in the matter?

God did not create us to serve money; He created money to serve us. We who love God and have a burden for the Gospel to be preached in the whole Earth should be the most blessed people.

God doesn't demand anything of you that He doesn't give you the ability to perform. He wants you to use that seed He has placed in your hand to prove Him and His Word. "Prove to Me that you love Me and trust Me," He is saying.

It doesn't seem possible, but I have known people who loved God and yet were somehow unable to trust Him with their money. What can they expect from Him?

There are several important points that I have discovered that can help you be blessed as a sower of the seed:

1. You must have a seed.
2. You must know the soil where you are planting that seed, and the right time for that planting.

**113**

3. You must know the time of your harvest.

Where I came from, we always ate everything fresh. You could go to the back of the house and gather bananas, oranges, papayas and other fresh fruits, but they were not always available. The harvest was controlled by the growing seasons, and that is true everywhere. There is a proper time to plant, and there is a proper time to harvest.

If you plant your seed at the wrong time of the year, it simply won't grow. There is a season for planting.

How can I know spiritually when the season for planting is right? There is a prompting in my spirit. Often, when you feel that prompting, what you have in your pocket or purse may be your last money, and the devil sneers, "Come on! You cannot give that money. You have many bills to pay. Be reasonable. Think of your family."

The Bible says:

*He that observeth the wind shall not sow; and he that regardeth the clouds shall not reap.* Ecclesiastes 11:4

Something hinders you, and you keep your money, failing to sow your seed. Consequently, you miss your harvest. Many say, "I don't know what happened to me." I know what happened. You failed to sow your seed or you didn't plant it in the right season. What did you expect?

I have actually seen those who had been millionaires and multimillionaires living like paupers because when God tested them, by putting seed in their hand, they failed to use it properly. They ate their seed, and now they are paying the price.

Prosperity and abundance were not man's ideas. God is not greedy, and He never complains about someone having too much.

If you were to go to the seashore and take out a few tankers full of water from the sea, would the sea complain? Of course not; there is plenty of water where that came from. And that's like God. He has an

**115**

inexhaustible supply, so that He does not mind you getting all that you need.

You would have to take out thousands of tankers full of water from the sea even to see a tiny drop in the water level. In the same way, God is the God of abundance. Abundance and blessing were His ideas. He said:

> *Beloved, I wish above all things that thou mayest prosper and be in health, even as thy soul prospereth.*
>
> 3 John 1:2

> *Let them shout for joy, and be glad, that favour my righteous cause: yea, let them say continually, Let the LORD be magnified, which hath pleasure in the prosperity of his servant.*
>
> Psalm 35:27

God's will for every man, woman, boy, and girl is abundance.

When God wanted to change the destiny of Abraham, He asked him to sow a seed.

When, the children of Israel were about to leave Egypt on their way to the Promised Land, God required a seed from them. Every family had to kill a lamb, a huge sacrifice for slave families. Lambs were a luxury for them. Many poor people around the world don't have a decent place to sleep at night, clean water to drink, or enough to eat for themselves and their children. A whole lamb would be a huge sacrifice.

Why would God require such a great sacrifice from His people? By this, He was saying, "If you will trust Me and kill a lamb, I will miraculously care for you for the next forty years." And He did!

Forty hours of labor a week cannot save you from the impending doom of poverty, lack, and constant attack from the kingdom of darkness. It takes the sowing of a seed.

Stop looking at your money as U.S. dollars (or whatever it is); look at it as seed. When you drop it into an offering bucket or wherever God shows you to sow it, see it falling as a seed into the ground and know that you have planted it in good soil. Say to yourself,

**117**

"I am planting, and there will come a time to reap what I have planted."

Whatever you do, don't repeat the lies of the enemy. "I am losing everything." "Everything is being stolen from me." "I have no hope for the future." If you love God and are doing His will, believe what He has said about you and speak that word, not the lies of the enemy.

He who sows will reap. It is guaranteed. Yes, you can experience *Heaven on Earth* right here and right now.

# CHAPTER 13

# WHY IS IT IMPORTANT NOT TO BE CONTROLLED BY MONEY?

*And when he was gone forth into the way, there came one running, and kneeled to him, and asked him, Good Master, what shall I do that I may inherit eternal life?* Mark 10:17

There are so many things that money cannot buy. It is something we all need, but we must not allow it to control us. A rich man came to Jesus. Kneeling down to greet Jesus and calling Him good was a welcome gesture, but much more was needed:

*And Jesus said unto him, Why callest thou me good? There is none good but one, that is, God. Thou knowest the commandments, do not commit adultery, do not kill, Do not steal, Do not bear false witness, Defraud not, Honour thy father and mother.*

*And he answered and said unto him, Master, all these have I observed from my youth.*

*Then Jesus beholding him loved him, and said unto him, one thing thou lackest: go thy way, sell whatsoever thou hast, and give to the poor, and thou shalt have treasure in heaven: and come, take up the cross, and follow me. And he was sad at that saying, and went away grieved: for he had great possessions.*

Mark 10:18-21

The man came to Jesus, began to tell Him how good He was and then proceeded to relate how he had kept all the commandments. He didn't steal. He didn't commit adultery. He was a very nice guy, but Jesus was not impressed. He said, "You are lacking one important thing."

Can you be rich and still suffer lack? Oh, yes! There are many things that money cannot buy. Any materially rich man who does not have the blessing of God on his life is seriously lacking.

The problem with our money is that we feel we own it, we deserve it, we earned it. Many cannot see the need to tithe to God because they somehow imagine that they have earned their money by the sweat of their own brow. Why should God have a portion of it? Why should He have the first portion of it?

It is only when you come to recognize that every blessing comes from above that tithing becomes easy, a joy to perform. If not, it is forever a chore.

Did God want this man's money? Absolutely not! God didn't need his money. He wanted to bless the man, to make sure he would never suffer lack. If God demands something of you, He is not robbing you. Just the opposite is true. He is protecting you from the thief.

If God asks something of you, joyfully give it and quickly. He has your best interests at heart and is planning to bless you mightily. However you earn your money, God is the one who provides for you. He provides us strength and ability to do our work so that we can earn. Without Him, we could do nothing.

What do you imagine would have happened had this rich man gone and sold everything he had and given to the poor? He certainly would not have starved to death. His family certainly would not have done without the necessities of life. God would have done miracles for them, just as He did for the children of Israel in the wilderness.

You cannot lose when you obey God. Therefore, if this man had sold everything he had and given to the poor, it would have guaranteed that he never again experienced lack of any kind.

That final verse is very sad indeed.

*And he was sad at that saying, and went away grieved: for he had great possessions.*

What does this man's sadness indicate? It reveals that He did not trust God. He believed the lies of the enemy. Instead of trusting God, he trusted his money and possessions. The most sad thing is that he missed out on the greatest blessings he could ever have imagined because he wasn't willing to trust and obey God.

We have no other information about this man's life, but you can be sure it was not a happy one. He was right to leave there in sadness. He had done a very sad thing, and could only look forward to sadness.

Many people talk about their "hard-earned" money. It was God Himself who gave you the strength to earn that money, the ability to earn it, and the job to earn it on. Give Him the glory He so richly deserves! And if He requires something of you, run to perform it. You cannot lose when you trust and obey God.

Many people enter into foolish business deals without consulting God. Then, when things go wrong, they want to blame Him or His servants or the Church. When you do business, it must be done with the right people, and it must be done in a way that is pleasing to God. If you do something foolish, why would you then think to blame God for the consequences?

In all of your business dealings, are you always careful to pay tithes on the blessings God sends your way? If not, can you blame Him if something goes wrong?

God must be our Source, or the money we have will lose its value. There is no room in our lives for more than one god, and money can very quickly become your god and rule your life.

Let today mark the end of poverty in your life. Agree with God. Let Him enrich your life in every way. You cannot make it on your own. It is not your job or your boss that provides for you. It is the supernatural hand of a loving God.

Have you prayed about your business ventures, listened to hear what God would say, and then obeyed what He told you? If not, what do you expect from God? He has the power to make your dollars (or other currencies) go further or to shrink their buying power. It's up to you to seek Him and obey Him.

You could receive any number of raises on your job, but if you are not honoring God in all that you do, something will always go wrong, and you will never have enough. If you learn to trust God and obey Him with your finances, you will never do without. Yes, you can experience *Heaven on Earth* right here and right now.

CHAPTER 14

# WHY IS GIVING SUCH AN IMPORTANT KEY TO PROSPERITY?

*Give, and it shall be given unto you; good measure, pressed down, and shaken together, and running over, shall men give into your bosom. For with the same measure that ye mete withal it shall be measured to you again.*

Luke 6:38

The promise of the Bible is clear. God is ready to give you more than you can ask or think. Are you ready to listen to His voice and obey His every command?

The planting is important, and planting in the right season is just as important. When the Spirit of the Lord is prompting you, don't dare refuse. Obey! Giving is a major key to God's blessings.

*Give* ... that's your part. What are you to give? Your seed. What will be the result? *"It shall be given unto you, good measure, pressed down, and shaken together, and running over shall men give unto you bosom."*

Who will give unto your bosom? Men. How will they give to you? Leave that to God. If you have been struggling, God says, "This is not the life I desire for you." Believe it and move into financial prosperity.

The late Oral Roberts, a great man of God, told the story of trusting the Lord to do a work in Africa. He contacted several Christian doctors who had recently graduated from his university in Tulsa, Oklahoma, hoping that they would accompany him on this venture. The doctors told him they would love to go, but they could not because they had student loans they needed to repay.

Dr. Roberts prayed and asked God what to do. He was directed to help the doctors repay their loans. He asked how much the loans were and came up with a total of $8 million that needed to be paid. He immediately set to work to raise that amount.

In a rather short time, Brother Roberts was able to raise $7 million, but that last million dollars seemed to be very hard to raise. In the end, the money came to him in one check, and it was from one man, an unbeliever.

Don't worry about where the money you need will come from. Let God do what He will. Don't limit Him in any way. God's promise is real. Sow your seed, and then expect your harvest.

I had an experience some years ago in New York. I was having a meeting in that great city, and I arrived early one evening to pray. There were about eight of us there, including the man who was hosting the conference. When a strange man came in, everybody was looking at him. He asked, "Who is the pastor here?"

My host pointed at me and said, "That's the pastor over there."

The man came over to me and again asked, "Are you the pastor?"

I said, "Yes, I am the pastor," wondering what was on the man's mind.

He put his hand in his pocket and brought out a fat envelope. Handing it to me, he said, "My name is Mohammed. I have a business over there [he pointed nearby] and something told me to bring this money to you."

Did I receive the money? Of course I did.

Stop making God so small. Can you trust your employer that he will pay you when payday comes, but you can't trust the Creator of the Universe, the Maker of Heaven and Earth? Trust your seed into His hands, and say, "Here, Lord. I will be back to receive my harvest," and begin to thank Him for it.

Why is giving so important to your financial prosperity? When you give back to God, it shows that you recognize who He is. He is God, and you are not God. He is King, and you are not King. He is the Creator of all things and when you honor Him, He is pleased.

Now that does not mean that God needs your money. Believe me, He doesn't. Your gift to Him is a sign of your appreciation and thankfulness for His goodness, for all that He has done for you, and for His great promises. His response is to open the windows of Heaven and pour you out blessings that there shall not be room enough to receive. Yes, you can experience *Heaven on Earth* right here and right now.

# CHAPTER 15

# WHY IS IT IMPORTANT TO RECOGNIZE THE GRACE OF GOD?

*Therefore let no man glory in men. For all things are your's; whether Paul, or Apollos, or Cephas, or the world, or life, or death, or things present, or things to come; all are your's; and ye are Christ's; and Christ is God's.*

1 Corinthians 3:21-23

The way God operates has not changed from the Old Testament to the New. Godly kings of the Old Testament, when they went out to battle, expected to win because God was with them. Godly businessmen of the Old Testament expected to prosper because God was with them. Whether you are in politics, the military, the marketplace, or the medical and professional fields, the expectation is the same. God has destined you to prosper, and He will do everything to make it happen.

Are you a teacher, an accountant, a computer programmer? If you love God and trust Him, He will prosper your way.

Whatever you feel called to in life, God is not expecting you to succeed on your own. Just as He annointed the priests and prophets of old to do their work, He also anointed other godly men and women for their particular calling.

Once you understand the love of God, His divine plan for your life, and what the grace of God has already provided for you, you will walk in victory, with an assurance in your heart and without fear of any kind.

You are mortal, but you can walk free of guilt once you know that everything that pertains to life and godliness has already been provided for you. It is yours ... when you know the grace that is given to you.

You and I both know that we don't deserve the favor of God and have done nothing to merit it. God just gives it to us because He loves us. Therefore, we can walk in favor without having to be constantly wondering what we have to do next to maintain it. Just as His love has brought us to this point, His love will carry us through.

The world will insist that we are not qualified for such blessing, but when God qualifies you, there is nothing any man or woman alive can do to stop it.

The grace of God has brought all things our way, but it is within our power to accept them or to reject them. Isaiah prophesied:

> *For this is as the waters of Noah unto me: for as I have sworn that the waters of Noah should no more go over the earth; so have I sworn that I would not be wroth with thee, nor rebuke thee. For the mountains shall depart, and the hills be removed; but my kindness shall not*

> *depart from thee, neither shall the cov-*
> *enant of my peace be removed, saith the*
> *Lord that hath mercy on thee.*
>
> Isaiah 54:9-10

What did God say? That He would never be angry with you, that no matter what you think you have done against Him, He will never rebuke you. That's enough to make any of us want to shout and jump for joy.

God said, "No matter what you do, My kindness will never depart from you." Everything that comes to me comes on the platform of God's mercy, not on the plat-form of my good works. When you have an understanding like that, you will live differently. You perceive life very differ-ently than others because you know, by the covenant you have with God, that you have a Shepherd watching over your life.

Jesus said:

> *I am the good shepherd: the good shep-*
> *herd giveth his life for the sheep.*
>
> John 10:11

The Good Shepherd is ready to do whatever is necessary to get His sheep safely to where they need to go. He will assure that all the wolves and other predicators lurking along the way are destroyed. We are His sheep, and He is a good shepherd. Therefore, He will gladly lay down His life for us.

David sang:

*Thou preparest a table before me in the presence of my enemies, thou anointest my head and my cup runneth over.*
Psalm 23:5

This shows me that an enemy is no longer my problem. The One who invited me to come and sit at His table will take care of any enemy. He was aware of the enemies around me when He prepared the table for me, and enemies are no problem for Him.

This is the security our covenant offers us. My Shepherd is alive and active. There is a table prepared for me, and it is filled with good things: long life, sound health, prosperity, goodness, mercy, and the grace of God. These are all on the table awaiting me.

Many people are angry and don't know where to turn. They try to fight their way out of life's battles, but they don't have enough strength. Meanwhile God has promised:

> *He suffered no man to do them wrong:*
> *yea, he reproved kings for their sakes;*
> *saying, Touch not mine anointed, and*
> *do my prophets no harm.*
>
> Psalm 105:14-15

Many are deeply depressed these days because of their needs. For the believer, the resolution of our needs is part of our citizenship.

Of course, money is not the answer. No matter what you think you know and no matter how much money you earn, you will be frustrated. Without money, however, there is no peace, and if there is no peace, then there can be fear. If there is fear, then there is torment. And if there is torment, death comes.

I have discovered that more than thirty percent of the American people are on antidepressant medications. Why would that be? It seems that something is telling them that things are not working. They try to pay their bills, they try to solve their problems, and the harder they try the more problems keep popping up.

One moment, they are saying, "Father, thank You that I am out from under this problem," and the next moment another problem is waiting to take its place. Eventually they become so depressed they have to take a medication. If you don't want to join them, you had better heed what I am saying here.

From the time we are born on this Earth, we hear many things from our parents, things they learned from their parents, and their parents learned it from their grandparents. The result is that we are firmly set in cultural ideas and ways of thinking, to an extent that we have lost touch with the originality of how to live. If you look at a copy of something for a long time, the original begins to look fake to you.

When Jesus Christ came to earth, people felt that His message was somehow blasphemous. What He said was so far removed from their set patterns of thinking that they could not understand what He was saying. His words had be filtered through their cultural makeup. He offended their religious sensibilities. They accused Him of being a man who was trying to make Himself God. He, of course, was telling them the truth, but their "truth" was different.

Be careful. You can become so comfortable with a problem or a limitation that you accept it as your destiny. Our Lord Jesus calls us to come out of the confusion of this world into the light of His glorious presence, into full freedom and fellowship with Him, the King of Glory. Yes, you can experience *Heaven on Earth* right here and right now.

# CHAPTER 16

# WHY IS IT IMPORTANT TO UNDERSTAND THE BLESSING?

*And God said let us make man in our own image after our likeness and let them have dominion over the fish of the sea, fowl of the earth, the cattle and over all creatures of the earth.* Genesis 1:26

Man (including woman) could not have dominion unless he had something inside of him put there by God so that he could do the job required. It would have been wicked of God to throw you into such an arena, tell you to dominate, and not give you the tools needed to do it.

However, there is nothing hard for God. He is blessed and from Him flows all blessing. God is so blessed that He can do anything without asking for help, and He has passed that blessing along to us.

The Bible declares:

*Blessed be the God the father of our Lord who hath blessed us with every spiritual blessings in heavenly places in Christ Jesus.* Ephesians 1:3

God is blessed, and that's why and how He blesses us. You cannot give what you don't have. God is the Blesser because He is the Blessed.

When man was created and given an assignment, he needed a force to operate in his office, and God provided it. To the average Christian, one who reads the Bible by just flipping through the pages, the thought of man having dominion over the Earth may seem farfetched. But consider the fact that God breathed the breath of life into man, and man became a living soul. Just as God had breathed into man, man then breathed into the animal kingdom.

In Genesis 1:28, a wonderful thing happened. The Bible says:

*And God blessed them.*   Genesis 1:28

This word *blessed* is not what you say to people when they sneeze. The biblical word *blessing* means "to be empowered." So, when the Bible says, *"And God blessed them,"* it means that He released a force into their lives that made them fruitful. They were then able to multiply and replenish the earth. They then subdued every creature and dominated the Earth.

Adam and Eve did nothing to deserve this power and authority. It was given to them by God because of His grace. From the moment His grace came upon man, he was able to rule the Earth. Why? Because the same force that was in God was now in him.

*Blessing* was not just a greeting. It was a dynamic force, and this same force was in operation in the life of Noah. The Bible says of him:

> *And God blessed Noah and his sons*
> *and he said unto them, be fruitful and*
> *multiply and replenish the earth.*
>
> Genesis 9:1

Just as God had said, it happened. There was no central bank, and Wall Street was not yet in existence, but they were blessed.

I have heard people say, "You don't know my situation." Well, what is your situation? I would say maybe you talk too much. All you need to do to change your status is to activate the blessing of God over your life.

The blessing of God is not related to the kind of job you have. When God blessed Noah, there was nothing on the Earth at all. It had all been destroyed by the Great Flood. Still, the blessing of God came upon Noah:

> *And the fear of you shall be upon every*
> *beast of the earth and every fowl of the*
> *earth and that moveth upon the earth*
> *and upon the fishes of the earth and thy*
> *hand they are delivered.*    Genesis 9:2

In other words, God was saying, "Nothing on this Earth will be able to intimidate you because I have put a force in you, and that force is enough to take care of you in every situation. You can rule the Earth in My power."

What does this mean? It means that if God put man into a desert, because of the force on the man, that desert would soon become a fruitful field. The force of God on the woman would convert that desert into a wonderful place to live.

You don't have to worry about who likes you and who doesn't like you because your blessing does not depend on other people. The only thing you need to be an overcomer is what God has already placed inside of you. His blessing is your victory in every sense of the word.

Because of the force of the blessing God releases on man, He said, nothing will be permitted to hurt you. The brothers of Joseph hated him and made a plan to take his life. If it had not been for the blessing of God upon him, they surely would have killed him.

They did throw him into a pit, and that alone is enough to kill some. With all the humiliations Joseph went through, he could very easily have suffered from depression. He was wrongly imprisoned, and lost years of his life in that place, and yet he was still in charge.

If that had been some of us, we would have turned our anger against God, and that would have made His angels disappear. This man Joseph was rejoicing, to an extent that even the other prisoners noticed it. He could rejoice because he had recognized the blessing that was upon his life and was concentrating on that, not the challenges he faced every day.

In the end, because of his faithfulness and excellence, Joseph was made head over all the other prisoners. He even became a counselor to the jailors. If there was any problem in the prison, everyone looked to Joseph for answers, and he had them:

We read in Isaiah:

> *Thus saith the* Lord, *As the new wine is found in the cluster, and one saith,*

*Destroy it not, for a blessing is in it: so will I do for my servants sakes, that I may not destroy them all.*   Isaiah 65:8

If the blessing is upon you, no man can destroy you. Don't let the challenges of life make you change. Instead, change the circumstances around you.

There is no way that the man called Isaac would have gotten the kind of result he got in his day, if it had not been for something extraordinary that was happening in his life. It was the blessing of God. The Bible clearly shows this:

*Then Isaac sowed in that land and received in the same year an hundred folds and the Lord blessed him. And the man waxed greater, and went forward, and grew until he became very great: For he had possession of hears, and great store of servants, and the Philistines envied him.*                Genesis 26:12-14

Was this blessing there because Isaac had certain people working for him? No! Was it because he had studied the climate? No! Was it because he was such a very good agriculturalist or knew and used the best seeds and methods? No! The weather was clearly not favorable to him, but the blessing came anyway.

The blessing of God will not permit anything you put your hand to to die. All that you touch will live. When God called Abraham, He didn't offer him a big check. He gave him something much better—the blessing:

> *Now the LORD had said unto Abram, get thee out of thy country, and from thy kindred and from thy father's house unto a land I will show thee, and I will make of thee a great nation, and I will bless thee, and make thy name great, and thou shall be a blessing: and I will bless them that bless and curse him that curseth thee, and in thee shall all families of the earth be blessed.* Genesis 12:1-3

Because we are the children of Abraham by faith, that is our connection to the blessing:

*Unto you first God having raised up his son Jesus, sent him to bless you.*

Acts 3:26

What connection could we possibly have with Abraham and his blessing? The mind of God was not just to make Abraham a ruler in the Earth; His mind was to make every man and woman in Christ Jesus to be fruitful, to multiply, to subdue, and to dominate the Earth.

God is ready to empower you in the same way He empowered Adam:

*Blessed be the God the father of our Lord who hath blessed us with every spiritual blessings in heavenly places in Christ Jesus.* Ephesians 1:3

The essence of this blessing is to terminate every sorrow and every pain in your life and to fill your life with every rich thing. This is not your job. God Himself has done it.

*The blessing of the Lord, it maketh rich,
and he addeth no sorrow with it.*

Proverb 10:22

The assignment of the blessing of the Lord is to make you rich. Do you know what the word *rich* means? It means "abundantly supplied." And, with this abundant supply, God adds no sorrow.

The Greek word translated *sorrow* can also be translated as "painful toiling." That was what Peter was referring to when he said to Jesus, *"We have toiled all night, and have taken nothing"* (Luke 5:5). These humble fishermen were sorrowful because they had worked all night and had nothing to show for it. Things were not working out for them. But they were about to be blessed and would soon experience a turnaround.

You cannot be blessed and have sorrow at the same time. It doesn't matter where you are placed or what you are working on, you can make things happen. You are a person who can make things work. You are an asset, never a liability.

Your boss should be celebrating you because you are bringing light in that place. That company will not go under while you are there because of the blessing upon your life. It is the mighty hand of Jehovah working on your behalf.

You cannot have Jehovah living inside of you and anything or anyone on this Earth contesting your success.

Some say, "But there are so many people attacking me." No, you are attacking yourself. The promise of God for you is:

*If God be for us, who can be against us?*                        Romans 8:31

It is not because you know a bishop that God is working in your life. It is because Jesus Christ died for you. If you can know that He died for you, your story will change.

Many time we see promises in the Scriptures, and we know they are ours, and we don't know why they are not working,. Well, you need to do something to activate those promises.

When God was giving a charge to the children Israel, He said:

> *For the* LORD *thy God bringeth thee into a good land, a land of brooks of water, of fountains and depths that spring out of valleys and hills: a land of wheat and barley, and vines, and fig trees, and pomegranates; a land of olive oil, and honey: a land wherein thou shalt eat bread without scarceness, thou shalt not lack any thing in it; a land whose stones are iron, and out of whose hills thou mayest dig brass: when thou has eaten and art full, thou shalt bless the* LORD *thy God for the good land which he hath given thee: beware that thou forget not the* LORD *thy God, in not keeping his commandments, and his judgments and his statutes, which I commanded thee this day.*        Deuteronomy 8:7-11

One cause for the blessing not working in your life may be that you have put God in second place. If God is number two in your life, you are in trouble. He warned His people not to forget Him or what He had done. The moment you forget, the blessing will stop working.

If you have to struggle to be blessed, something's wrong. If you are struggling, how are you different from the heathen? Jesus said:

> *Therefore take no thought, saying, What shall we eat? or, What shall we drink? or, Wherewithal shall we be clothed? (For after all these things do the Gentiles seek:) for your heavenly Father knoweth that ye have need of all these things. But seek ye first the kingdom of God, and his righteousness; and all these things shall be added unto you.* Matthew 6:31-33

You don't have to struggle. Some people say, "We will fast and pray that God supplies our need." Fasting and prayer are good, but you were not meant to struggle in life. God just wants you to bring your requests to Him in faith, and He will act on your behalf. It's that simple.

Some come to God with tears of sorrow, but He doesn't respect your tears. He respects your faith. If you are like many, they only come to God when they need something from Him. I know people I only see in church when they are experiencing some sort of challenge in life. Otherwise, they never appear.

If you asked them, they would say, "Yes, I am a member of the church," but their commitment has no depth. Why should God prosper them? If He cannot be number one in your life, then He doesn't want to be on your list.

You will have the blessing when you seek first the Kingdom of God, when God is a part of your daily life, when God is part of your program, when God is in charge of your finances, where God is in your thinking. That is what shows me you are seeking Him first.

Some people think, "Why should I be in church every Sunday; I'm not a pastor, and I don't plan to be one." Well, that's why things have not been working in your life the way they should. For far too many, I can tell that Satan is standing nearby, and he is rubbing their back and convincing them that it is better to serve him.

If God is not in His proper place in your life, that's very dangerous. Whether you know it or not, you are under attack 24/7. Paul the apostle wrote:

> *For a great door and effectual is opened unto me, and there are many adversaries.* 1 Corinthians 16:9

This was a man with a close relationship with God. He had experienced God's grace, and yet he had many adversaries.

If prayer is a problem for you, then Satan may be sleeping in the same bed. How dangerous! God must be given His rightful place.

The world around us seems to be getting more and more wicked. It is because Satan is revealing himself. Sadly, many Christians are taking their orders from the world, not from God.

There were no pastors in my family, but my family members all knew that they could not get me to renounce my call. I was very stubborn for God, and it paid off.

Don't depend on a person, an aunt or uncle, for instance. One day they will die, and what will you do then? If your hope has been in them, you will be lost. If you don't have a personal experience, an encounter with God, you will be in serious trouble. No man lives forever. Only one is eternal, and His name is Jesus. Your commitment to him is the key to your enlargement. Seek Him first.

In the time of King Asa, it is recorded:

*And they entered into a covenant to seek the LORD God of their fathers with all their heart and with all their soul: That whosoever would not see seek the LORD God of Israel should be put to death, whether small or great, whether man or woman: And they sware unto the LORD with a loud voice, and with shouting, and with trumpets, and with cornets:*

*and all Judah rejoiced at the oath, for they had sworn with all their heart, and sought him with their whole desire; and he was found of them: and the LORD gave them rest round about.*

2 Chronicles 15:12-15

When I was a young boy in ministry, it seemed it was reserved for those who wanted to suffer. In fact, the moment you said that God had called you, the people would say, "Yeah, God got this one too." When I came out of college with a good degree, first in my class, and I told my friends and family that God had called me, they all looked at me like I was crazy, and then they said it: "You are sick." This resulted in much persecution because people around me were sure that I was losing my mind.

People would tell me, "So and so person did not prosper in ministry." I had to answer, "I am not looking for money; I am looking for Him who called me." I said to God, "Don't let anything work for me if I fail to obey You in this call."

157

I didn't know that a pastor could own a house. Where I was raised, pastors never had their own car, so I didn't aspire to those things. I was entering into ministry to serve God, I was committed to Him, and He knew that.

Where is your heart? Some Christians, when they have to go to church, are dragging their feet. They put everything else ahead of God and then wonder why they are not blessed. "Oh, but I simply have to take my children on vacation to Disney World," they say. Well, there is nothing wrong with going to see Mickey Mouse, but do it at the right time. Get your priorities right. If things are not working for you, this may be the reason. What place does God have in what you are doing?

We even have people committed to the local church but not to God. The result is that they live in fear. They see wrong in everything and are very easily offended. If you are committed, what others do doesn't affect you. Your eyes are fixed on God. Get your priorities in order.

Zechariah urged the people of his day to change their way of thinking. When they did, God gave them rest round about:

> *And he sought God in the days of Zecha-riah, who had understanding in the vision of God: and as long as he sought the LORD, God made him to prosper.*
>
> 2 Chronicles 26:5

Prosperity is attached to seeking first the Kingdom. If you are willing, blessings are coming your way. Yes, you can experience *Heaven on Earth* right here and right now.

# PART II

# Looking in the Mirror

# CHAPTER 17

# YOUR BLESSING IS HERE

*But we all, with open face beholding
as in a glass the glory of the Lord, are
changed into the same image from glory
to glory, even as by the Spirit of the
Lord.*                          2 Corinthians 3:18

Just as looking in the mirror gives you
a reflection of who you are physically, so
the Word of God is a reflection of your
true self, your spirit man. Man is a triune
being. Originally a spirit, he has a soul,
and he dwells in a body. The only parts
we usually focus on are the mind and
the body. That's why we go to school.
Mankind is always seeking to develop the
mind and equip it.

Our other focus is the body. That's why many go to the gym, to build their muscles and develop their body. Too many think that's all there is to man, but that's a lie from the pit of Hell. God wants your mind and spirit to be renewed so that you become effective as a new creature or new creation, as some translations of the Bible word it:

> *Therefore if any man be in Christ, he is a new creature: old things are passed away; behold, all things are become new.* 2 Corinthians 5:17

This scripture is not talking about your physical body or your mind; it's talking about your spirit. Your spirit looks exactly like Jesus. When you are born again, it's your spirit man that has new birth.

> *And the very God of peace sanctify you wholly; and I pray God your whole spirit and soul and body be preserved blameless unto the coming of our Lord Jesus Christ.* 1 Thessalonians 5:23

The more you look at the mirror (which is the Word of God), the more it will show you exactly the way you really look, and the more you look at it, the more you will become like the picture you're looking at.

If you judge yourself, class yourself, or evaluate yourself based on what your body is telling you or based on what you are thinking, you may be confused about who you are. What you see in the Word of God is a practical picture of who you are through the redemption Christ purchased for us on Calvary.

When you gave your life to Jesus, something happened on the inside. You are now sinless, and you cannot become sick or oppressed or die prematurely. You're stronger than your body or mind would lead you to believe. You have been born again, born from above.

*But he that is joined unto the Lord is one spirit.*          1 Corinthians 6:17

Declare it: "I am joined unto the Lord; I am one spirit with Him, for God's Word has

**165**

said it." If you're joined with the Lord and are one spirit with Him, then you are expected to manifest the same result He had. Nothing less must be your achievement.

While Jesus was still here on Earth, He said to those who loved Him:

> *Verily, verily, I say unto you, He that believeth on me, the works that I do shall he do also; and greater works than these shall he do; because I go unto my Father.* John 14:12

Since this is God's Word, God said you can do the same works and even greater works than Jesus. There's nothing terminal when it comes to your case. There's nothing that can be called impossible when it comes to your case. There's nothing that can be called failure when it comes to your case. There's nothing that can be called obstacle when it comes your case. Why? Because the same power, grace, and anointing that was upon Jesus is now upon you. You are joined together with Jesus.

Before Jesus left the Earth, He told His disciples certain things. Among them, He said:

> *Then said Jesus to them again, Peace be unto you: as my Father hath sent me, even so send I you.* John 20:21

Do you know that I am sent just as Jesus was sent? If you are sent like Jesus was sent, then why is that two fish and five loaves remain in your hands for long periods without any increase? Why is it that embarrassment is killing you? Why do you allow situations to prevail over you? You are sent just like Jesus was sent.

> *For if by one man's offence death reigned by one; much more they which receive abundance of grace and of the gift of righteousness shall reign in life by one, Jesus Christ.* Romans 5:17

You and I have received an abundance of grace, and Jesus is the proof that we must reign here on Earth. We are sent to this world to reign over situations, to reign over sickness, poverty, affliction, barrenness, and sin. You have a mandate to reign over Satan himself. Why? Because you have received an abundance of grace and the gift of righteousness.

The Church has not been able to master this issue of righteousness. Righteousness is not the good things you do; it's a gift. God gave you His own position, and He took your position. He knew you couldn't fix things or do what needed to be done. He took your weaknesses and gave you His strengths.

Did you know that you deserve to have answers to all your prayers? Did you know that you deserve to be healed of every ailment? Did you know you ought to be healthy and wealthy, able to give to others in need? Why? Calvary means that it's all been paid for. It's not because you fast and pray more than others. You fast and pray because you know it's yours. The grace Jesus gave you makes it compulsory for you to labor more than others.

For example, if you were to go for a job interview, and the recruiter came to your house the night before and gave you the questions to be asked and told you how to dress and how to speak and address each question when asked, would you be eager to go for the interview or would you run away?

If they say the interview will be at 9:00 AM, you will be there by 6:30, and even before that you are already testifying in church about your victory. You have not yet attended the interview, but the interviewer has already told you everything you need to know about the job.

In the same way, grace has made everything available, and grace has told you the end result, so you have nothing to fear. This grace the Bible speaks of is sometimes defined as "undeserved favor." If you had to deserve it, you would never see it.

We have a wrong concept about our person, about our identity, about our righteousness. We have a wrong concept about what grace is all about. The result is that we struggle for what Calvary has already provided. We treat the Word of God as if it was only sent to Abraham. Until we begin to see God's Word as His personal love letter to us, we will not enjoy the prosperity it promises.

I am always excited about going to church because I am looking forward to hearing God speak to me directly. I don't need anyone to be my intermediary. I can hear God for myself. When the Word is being preached, God shows me how I look in His presence. Others may not like my look, but He likes it. He said:

> *He that spared not his own Son, but delivered him up for us all, how shall he not with him also freely give us all things?* Romans 8:32

Declare, "I have everything." If you believe it and declare it, it will be yours.

When you begin to see the Word of God as God speaking to you directly, affecting every area of your life, it will soon rule everything about you. When you have an understanding of your identity in Christ, you will dare to do exploits, knowing that you can do everything that Jesus could do. Your spirit man now understands that, and it makes everything possible to you.

It's your mind that's deceiving you when the thought comes to you that you are not up to the task. You can do everything that Jesus can do.

> *I can do all things through Christ which strengtheneth me.*    Philippians 4:13

If you don't believe this, it doesn't mean that God has changed His mind. If He says *"greater works than these shall ye do,"* He is able to do it through you and through me.

Jesus was embarrassed by His disciples because what He had empowered them to do they could not. He said to them:

> *Because strait is the gate, and narrow is the way, which leadeth unto life, and few there be that find it.*    Matthew 7:14

**171**

*And when he had called unto him his twelve disciples, he gave them power against unclean spirits, to cast them out, and to heal all manner of sickness and all manner of disease.*

Matthew 10:1

Even after Jesus had given the disciples authority and power, they didn't know why and didn't know what they could or should do with it. The fact that they didn't believe they could do it caused Jesus to feel bad about it. In fact, He rebuked them sharply:

*And I brought him to thy disciples, and they could not cure him. Then Jesus answered and said, O faithless and perverse generation, how long shall I be with you? how long shall I suffer you? bring him hither to me.*

Matthew 17:16-17

Jesus felt so bad that He called His beloved followers *"a faithless and perverse generation."* After all, He had given them everything they needed for life, everything they needed to survive and thrive. It was not as if they couldn't do it. It was just because they *didn't* do it.

If I asked you to go and minister healing to someone in need and you refused, believing that I alone could do it, it would mean that you believed Jesus died for me, but not for you. When you come in contact with sick people, the thought comes to you that you don't have the anointing, that you're not righteous enough. The truth is very different. Jesus said:

> *I am the vine, ye are the branches: He that abideth in me, and I in him, the same bringeth forth much fruit: for without me ye can do nothing.*
>
> John 15:5

Without Him we can do nothing, and yet Jesus ended this teaching by calling these same men to be His witnesses:

> *But when the Comforter is come, whom I will send unto you from the Father,*

> *even the Spirit of truth, which pro-*
> *ceedeth from the Father, he shall testify*
> *of me: and ye also shall bear witness,*
> *because ye have been with me from the*
> *beginning.*                     John 15:26-27

When He says to us, "Go," why not go? Is it God who has changed, or are we the ones who have changed?

Are you thinking of your unrighteousness? Are you worried about your inability and not appreciating the ability of Almighty God in you? Have you lost the understanding of your destiny?

I have a very big and heavy shelf in my office. One morning, while I was bathing, preparing for our Sunday morning service, the Holy Spirit spoke to me. He said, "If you asked someone to go and move that shelf, what do you think that person would say? It's so big and heavy that he would probably say, 'I'm sorry but I can't do it because it's so big and heavy.' But what if you got five strong men to go help the first man you asked to do the moving? Together, they could get the job done without any trouble. Well, you have an Helper now. The Holy Spirit is right beside you and in you. Enough of the tears in your life! By the authority of the name of Jesus, you are taking over.

"But, if the five hefty men came to help, and the first guy saw them and ran away because he was afraid, if you later asked him, 'Have you moved that shelf?' he would have to answer, 'No!' And why not? Because when he saw the five hefty men, he was frightened and ran away. This is a problem of trust. He didn't trust me enough to know that I care for him and because I care for him, I sent those men to help him. If he trusted me, he wouldn't look at their size. He would not be intimidated by their appearance because I sent them."

When situations and circumstances come your way, trust God that these things cannot overpower you. Stop looking at the situations. Instead, look to the One who sent you. You are not a man or woman under experiment; you were sent here with a purpose, just like Jesus to rule and reign.

Human faith is always looking for evidence in the physical, but Jesus' faith doesn't need it. Jesus' faith is always looking to Jesus for the end result. You can cast out devils and raise the dead. After all, you are not doing it in your own name. You're the one speaking, but there is another One doing the work. Why should you be afraid to speak to cancer? Declare, "Cancer, I command you in the name of Jesus, come out."

A lady came to me just a few weeks ago and told me that doctors had given her only a short time to live. Her son had also died from cancer. I told her that these stories were not in the Bible, that she didn't have to die, and that with God's help, we could fix the situation.

She insisted that she was totally unworthy of God's blessing, that He had been disappointed with her. She was intended to be in ministry, but she wasn't doing what she had been called to do. Her conclusion was that all this was the reason for her suffering.

"Come on, my dear," I said, "God is not punishing you because of what you did. Even those who think they have done their best, when it is analyzed, we can find some flaws. God is asking you to depend on His righteousness, not on your good behavior. Our very best is still crude in God's eyes."

Together, we read some passages of scripture, and then I commanded the cancer to come out of her. When she went to the hospital, they said they couldn't find any more cancer. Whatever is threatening your life, I curse it now in the name of Jesus.

We're not using *our* faith anymore; we're using the faith of Jesus. We trust in His finished work and His ability:

> *Knowing that a man is not justified by the works of the law, but by the faith of Jesus Christ, even we have believed in Jesus Christ, that we might be justified by the faith of Christ, and not by the works of the law: for by the works of the law shall no flesh be justified.* Galatians 2:16

**177**

That bears repeating: we are *"justified by the faith of Christ, and not by the works of the law: for by the works of the law shall no flesh be justified."* Jesus Christ has faith, and it is His faith that we depend on. When God opened my eyes to see this truth, my faith dimension was enlarged. Because of the faith of Jesus, we can get anything from God anytime we need it.

The faith of Christ is ready for anything. It's ready for all impossibilities. Declare with me today, "I have the faith of the Son of God." This was the faith Jesus described when He said "have God's kind of faith. If you have My kind of faith, you will say to this mountain, "Move and be cast into the sea,' and nothing shall be impossible unto you" (see Mark 11:22-24).

Remember, the Bible says that the faith of Jesus will move any mountain anytime anywhere. The good news is that if you don't have a job, take your job now by the faith of Jesus, and do it in Jesus' name. I decree favor to rest upon you now. Take possession of your inheritance in God.

I have signed many employment letters, and people are hired. Before it happens physically, however, it must first happen spiritually. If you believe it will happen to you, please declare, "I have the faith of Jesus." This was the same faith the apostle Paul used. He didn't use his own faith, but the faith of Jesus:

> *I am crucified with Christ: nevertheless I live; yet not I, but Christ liveth in me: and the life which I now live in the flesh I live by the faith of the Son of God, who loved me, and gave himself for me.*
>
> Galatians 2:20

Paul lived by the faith of the Son of God, not the faith of Paul. I, too, live by the faith of Jesus, knowing that the faith of Jesus will get things for me from Father God every time. There is no closing time with God.

Peter used this same faith:

> *Simon Peter, a servant and an apostle of Jesus Christ, to them that have obtained*

**179**

> *like precious faith with us through the*
> *righteousness of God and our Saviour*
> *Jesus Christ.* 1 Peter 1:1

Peter had obtained *"like precious faith."* What kind of faith was that? It was the faith of Jesus. That was the faith he and John used at the Beautiful Gate when they saw the crippled man. When they released the faith of Jesus to him, the crippled man began walking, and leaping, and praising God.

How do you release this kind of faith? The moment you call on the name of Jesus, His faith is released. These disciples were not special people. They just knew what we all need to know. Life is filled with dangers, but when we know the truth, we can overcome it all.

If you want to get a new house, use the faith of Jesus. Do you want to get healed? Use the faith of Jesus. Whatever you want to do, use the faith of Jesus. Your own faith may not be enough to carry you to where you're going.

The moment you got born again, God gave you everything you will ever need.

You are clothed in Christ from your head to your toes. When Satan sees you, he doesn't know who is inside that armor—the armor of righteousness, topped off by the crown of glory. The moment he sees you, he says, "This is my Master, the One who died on the cross." Why does he say that? Because you look exactly like Jesus.

Until you speak, the devil will put pressure on you. Then, it's what you say that will let him know that the person inside the armor is not Jesus. The moment you start speaking doubt and fear, Satan will say, "Aha, Jesus didn't speak like this. Let me pursue this one because he's not Jesus. He's a fake."

When you have financial challenges, the first thing you say is, "I'm broke." The enemy will pressure you until you say it. He will attempt to block every avenue of blessing until you say it. Then, once he knows that the person inside is not Jesus, he will double his torments.

Jesus would never talk like that, and the reason you talk that way is that you don't know your true identity in Christ. Start speaking like Jesus did in the face of the storms of life. When everything seems to be collapsing, just declare, "Peace, be still!"

Your spirit understands that; it's only your mind that's telling you that you will be destroyed by life's storms. Your mind must get connected to your spirit through the Word, so that God can renew it.

When you receive a bad diagnosis from your doctor, declare, "Liver [or whatever part of your body is affected], hear the Word of the Lord. I speak to you in the name of Jesus Christ, 'Be repaired.' I speak to every infection in you and command it: 'Get out right now!'"

You're in charge here, so stop speaking what the devil is suggesting to you. When you say you have an infection in the bladder, the devil will say, "Yes, that's right. Receive it!" Satan is using your own authority against you.

When the devil is putting pressure on you, and you cannot seem to overcome it yourself, get to some person who knows how to speak the word of faith. Don't keep this to yourself. Seek help from a person who can say, "Let's stop this now because you have the faith of Jesus."

Are you aware that God Himself doesn't have anything against you? No matter where you are right now, His hands are stretched out to you to ensure that you don't fail. The Law was given to bring you to the end of yourself, but it could never make a person righteous.

The Law makes you guilty and causes you to cry out, "Lord, I need a Savior. I am dying, and Your Spirit was sent so that I would not be judged by everything written in the Law."

When you know how much you're loved by God, sin will become anathema to you. God promised:

> *For this is as the waters of Noah unto me: for as I have sworn that the waters of Noah should no more go over the earth; so have I sworn that I would not*

*be wroth with thee, nor rebuke thee. For the mountains shall depart, and the hills be removed; but my kindness shall not depart from thee, neither shall the covenant of my peace be removed, saith the LORD that hath mercy on thee.*

Isaiah 54:9-10

Isaiah 53 describes the suffering of Jesus in our place:

*Surely he hath borne our griefs, and carried our sorrows: yet we did esteem him stricken, smitten of God, and afflicted. But he was wounded for our transgressions, he was bruised for our iniquities: the chastisement of our peace was upon him; and with his stripes we are healed.* Isaiah 53:4-5

It is through the suffering of God's Son that we are justified. He went through that cruelty for you and me. It was not just the beatings by the Roman soldiers that made Him miserable. It was much more. He had to take upon Himself our punishment.

In a moment's time, the Father heaped upon Jesus all the sins of the whole world and all the sicknesses and diseases of the whole world. No wonder His form was so distorted that no one desired Him!

In that moment, Jesus not only bore all the sins and the punishment for the sins of every man, woman, boy, and girl of every generation. On top of this shame, He also had to suffer cancer, diabetes, strokes, heart disease, and every other human ailment all heaped upon Him at once.

The people of that day shamed Him, mocked Him, and, removing all His clothes, humiliated Him publicly. They spat upon Him. The spittle of a large number of soldier at once must have been like a vicious shower. They did it to spite Him, and no one came to His rescue.

Beloved, please don't neglect this massive payment Christ made through His sacrifice so that the enemy would not be able to torment you. Let today be the end of every oppression in your life through the faith of Jesus.

If you need a job, God has the perfect job waiting for you. One young man came for prayer to get a job. After we prayed, he left. On his way home, he met a friend who said he was going for an interview, so he accompanied him.

At the site of the interview, the managing director come out, saw him, and asked, "Young man, what are you doing here?"

He answered, "I'm just accompanying a friend who came for an interview."

"Don't you need a job?" he was asked. He said he did, so the managing director instructed the personnel manager to interview him. At the end of the day, he got the job, and the friend didn't. That's undeserved favor. Receive yours right now in Jesus' name. Now, that is *Heaven on Earth*.

# CHAPTER 18

# CHANGED INTO THE SAME IMAGE

*Now the Lord is that Spirit: and where the Spirit of the Lord is, there is liberty. But we all, with open face beholding as in a glass the glory of the Lord, are changed into the same image from glory to glory, even as by the Spirit of the Lord.* 2 Corinthians 3:17-18

Understanding the reality of the spirit world is the beginning of victory and blessing. This is because the spirit world controls the physical. The spirit world is the originator of the physical world. You belong to the spirit world but are manifesting in the physical world.

The physical aspect of man is the body that can be touched, but no one can touch the soul. Only the Word of God can reach in and touch the soul. That's why I can say a word to you, and you will laugh and jump, or I can speak to you, and you will start crying. I didn't touch you, but simply spoke to you, and a reaction occurred because I touched your soul. The soul is the center of emotion, reasoning, and thinking.

I repeat: No man can touch your spirit. The only thing that can touch your spirit is the Word of God. Jesus said:

> *It is the spirit that quickeneth; the flesh profiteth nothing: the words that I speak unto you, they are spirit, and they are life.* John 6:63

The problem with some believers is that they are living in the realm of the body and mind and not connecting with their spirits at all. Because of this anomaly, life becomes miserable for them. Why? Because all the information they live with and from is fake and not original.

The activities of your soul and body depend on your spirit. Your soul, or mind, and your body cannot be compared with your spirit. They are much like the wrapper on a piece of candy. I have never seen anyone eat the wrapper with the candy. There is no comparison.

If something doesn't profit you, how will you feel? If someone came to you and said, "You don't profit me in any way," would you say, "Amen"? What the person is saying is that you are simply useless.

The Bible says that the flesh (our body), which we pay so much attention to, does not profit us anything. Therefore, the flesh must not be allowed to dictate to our lives. What we feel and think is no answer to the questions of life. *"The flesh profiteth nothing."*

When you pick up a mirror and look into it, the image in the mirror looks like you, but that's not really you; it's just a reflection of who you are. What you have seen in the mirror is your reflection.

What you are seeing in the mirror is not a powerful description of yourself, but a mere reflection of how you look. Still, you believe it so much that before you go out, you take another look, make some adjustments, and then think, "Perfect!"

The mirror gives a reflection of who you are, it pleases you, and you don't argue about it. You also don't pray about it. No one has ever come to me with a request that because he's going to look into a mirror, he wants me to pray with him. I would treat such a request as a waste of my time. The image you see in the mirror is a physical reflection of your body, but the Word of God is a reflection of who you really are.

> *Now the Lord is that Spirit: and where the Spirit of the Lord is, there is liberty. But we all, with open face beholding as in a glass the glory of the Lord, are changed into the same image from glory to glory, even as by the Spirit of the Lord.* 2 Corinthians 3:17-18

The Word of God is the mirror that shows who you are. Therefore, if you want to know how you look, think of the Word of God. Whatever you see there is who you are.

What you see in the mirror is a reflection, but not the original you. That's why it's important for you to know that God didn't create you to be sick, poor, or afflicted.

Jesus lived in the reality of the spirit world and demonstrated His rule over every part of that world, including all sickness, Satan, and demons. Demons asked Him, "Are you here to torment us before our day?" (see Matthew 8:29). That's how powerful He was while He was here on Earth.

Jesus spoke to the Jews, telling them, *"Before Abraham was, I am"* (John 8:58). The people were confused by this statement. Surely this Jesus was not even fifty years old. How could He be older than Abraham? Of course, He was not talking about the Boy Jesus who was born in Bethlehem about thirty years earlier; He was talking about the real Jesus who was in the beginning with Father God and who created all things in conjunction with the Father.

> *And the Word was made flesh, and dwelt among us, (and we beheld his glory, the glory as of the only begotten of the Father,) full of grace and truth.*
>
> John 1:14

Jesus was talking about Himself as God, the Son. The people thought He was referring to Jesus, the son of Mary, so they couldn't understand Him.

Because of Jesus' response, the people wanted to stone Him. How could a man call Himself the Son of the living God? They were about to arrest Him, but He told His followers not to worry. Why? Because He wasn't alone. The Father was with Him.

To the people nearby, Jesus seemed to be alone. When you deal with people who are only conscious of their physical realities and their minds, they will run you down, if you're not careful. They cannot see the blessing, promotion, and victory you're talking about.

You may be talking about what has already been given to you in Christ, and to you that is very real because you have seen it in the Word of God. To others, this will seem like an absurdity.

The Bible says; "You shall be the head and not the tail" (see Deuteronomy 28:13). When you see that in the mirror of the Word, it doesn't matter what you have been told at work. Whatever happens, you are still the head.

When Christ was about to be crucified, He told His tormentors, "I could ask My Father right now, and He would give me twelve legions of angels" (see Matthew 26:53). Jesus was conscious of the spirit world. When He was told that Lazarus had died, He knew it was a fact, but He also knew what the Word of God said:

*The land of Zabulon, and the land of Nephthalim, by the way of the sea, beyond Jordan, Galilee of the Gentiles;*

> *the people which sat in darkness saw*
> *great light; and to them which sat in*
> *the region and shadow of death light is*
> *sprung up.*　　　　Matthew 4:15-16

The people who had sat in darkness had now seen a great light. To those sitting in the shadow of death, light had sprung up. Because He was in that territory, death could not reign there. When Jesus was brought before the tomb of Lazarus, He commanded death to go.

Amazingly, Lazarus had been dead already for four days. But even if he had been dead for twenty years, Christ could still have raised him up from the grave. Because He was in that territory, death could not reign there.

Jesus didn't mind the fact that by this time, the body of Lazarus was already stinking because of the natural decay that occurs after death. He was Lord over decay as well as death. Jesus knew who He was, so death and decay didn't stop Him.

One of the greatest attacks the enemy unleashes on the Church of Jesus Christ is in this matter of identity. We see this playing out in the book of John:

> *Then said Jesus to them again, Peace be unto you: as my Father hath sent me, even so send I you.*     John 20:21

Jesus knew His power because He was sent, and as we saw in the last chapter, I am sent, just like Jesus was sent. Therefore, nothing can stop me, as nothing could stop Him. Whatever couldn't stop Jesus can't stop me either.

There's no devil in Hell that can successfully attack you and me. No devil can stop us. Whatever couldn't stop Jesus cannot stop us either.

You cannot doubt what you see in the mirror, even though it is a reflection. Therefore, we must stop doubting what God's Word says about us. It is the real picture of who we are.

God's Word has been tried seven times and still maintains its purity. You can depend on it more than you can depend on any earthly mirror:

> *The words of the LORD are pure words:*
> *as silver tried in a furnace of earth, puri-*
> *fied seven times.*　　　Psalm 12:6

In the world of the spirit, the Word of God is the most powerful force in existence. The writer to the Hebrews declared that *"through faith we understand that the worlds were framed by the word of God":*

> *Through faith we understand that the*
> *worlds were framed by the word of God,*
> *so that things which are seen were not*
> *made of things which do appear.*
> 　　　　　　　　Hebrews 11:3

The Word of God is the raw material that makes things happen. God said, *"Let there be light,"* and what happened? *"There was light."* God placed the sun in the sky. And how was He able to hang it there? Explain it to the rest of us if you claim to know. How did the sun, moon, and stars become suspended in the heavens?

For millions of years that light has never blinked. The Lord hung it there, and it has remained there ever since, with no pillars to support it. God commanded it to stay there, and it obeyed His voice.

The Word of God is the most powerful force ever. The problem with some believers is that they don't know when God is speaking. God doesn't speak to our soul or mind; He speaks to the real you, your spirit.

You and I must read the Word of God, believe the Word of God, and lift up the Word of God to see the reflection of who we really are. After salvation, your real person, which is your spirit, comes alive, even though your body and mind remain the same. If you were stupid before being saved, it is time to stop being stupid. You can now become wise through Christ.

When you got saved, it was your spirit that got saved. If you were bald-headed before getting saved, don't expect that to change. Your head will still be bald like mine.

As soon as your spirit is reborn, it's in the same class with Jesus, and you receive an anointing because of that. But, because many depend only on the mind and body, which continues telling them to do things which are against the will of God, they cannot grow as quickly as they should:

> *Yet now he has reconciled you to himself through the death of Christ in his physical body. As a result, he has brought you into his presence and you are wholly and blameless as you stand before him without a single fault.* Colossians 1:22, NLT

The carnal mind has a hard time understanding the reality of the fact that it is impossible for our spirit to sin. The Bible says it very clearly:

> *Whosoever is born of God doth not commit sin; for his seed remaineth in him: and he cannot sin, because he is born of God.* 1 John 3:9

*"He cannot sin."* Your recreated spirit is now in the same class with God, but

because you are being controlled by your mind and body, you are standing against the dictates of your spirit. That's the reason many mess up. Thankfully, God has given us the opportunity to repent. Therefore, as soon as you sin, re-connect immediately back to God, who is your Source, and say, "Lord, I am sorry. I messed up." And that settles it. As far as God is concerned, you appear before Him without any fault whatsoever.

If you govern your life with doctrines and traditions, you will pull yourself continually downward. There are so many wrong doctrines in the world. But this we know: Jesus never came to condemn anyone. The Bible says:

*There is therefore now no condemnation to them which are in Christ Jesus, who walk not after the flesh, but after the Spirit.* Romans 8:1

How could this be? Because they are in the same level of spirit and mind with the Lord.

**199**

It's as if their sins were never committed. You can't be in the camp of success and still fail. We have *"put on the new man"*:

> *And that ye put on the new man, which after God is created in righteousness and true holiness.*     Ephesians 4:24

As difficult as it is for the mind to understand, when you become born again, you put on the new man. Therefore, the Bible calls you righteous. That means you're in right standing with God. It means equality with God to an extent that you can approach Him, as if you had never touched sin in your life.

Only grace could do that, and that is precisely why the grace of God came. When it came, it changed your life completely. Before redemption you were created from dust, but after salvation God re-created your spirit.

There are some scriptures you should ignore because they're not talking about you. One example is Genesis 3:19:

*For dust thou art, and unto dust shalt thou return.*

This was not for a new-creation believer in Christ. You are no more created in dust, but in righteousness and true holiness. There is also a false holiness, which came through the Law.

*Beloved, let us love one another: for love is of God; and every one that loveth is born of God, and knoweth God.*

1 John 4:7

God's Word equates you and me with Jesus. Your reborn spirit is so anointed, so powerful, and so intelligent that nobody can defeat you in battle. The problem is that your mind and body are against Him and cannot understand Him. Every time He gives you a word, your body says, "That's not possible," and your mind says, "How could you ever reason that out? The doctor's report is here to prove it."

One night, I had a long flight and wanted to use my iPad and computer to get some work and study done, but at thirty thousand feet, for some reason, both my computer and iPad refused to start up. It suddenly occurred to me, *If Jesus had been in my shoes, what would He have done?* I began to meditate on the spirit realm controlling the physical ... until I finally got agitated and spoke to the iPad, commanding it to "open."

I don't know what the person beside me thought about all of this, and I didn't really care. After all, it was *my* iPad, and I paid for the seat on the airplane. I declared: "Open ... now!" It opened, and I said, "Good boy."

What does all of this have to do with our subject? The fact is that God wants you and me to get out of the flesh and mind and begin to operate at the level of Jesus. I declare to you today: you will never go down anymore. Anything causing a limitation in your life is eternally removed in Jesus' name!

I am not saying these things because I am a bishop, but because I am born again. It also has everything to do with the reality of the spirit world. As we have seen, the spirit world controls everything here in the natural. If you want to base your life on what you see and what you think, you will run God down with your plans.

The Bible says, *"To be carnally minded is death; but to be spiritually minded is life and peace":*

> *For to be carnally minded is death; but to be spiritually minded is life and peace. Because the carnal mind is enmity against God: for it is not subject to the law of God, neither indeed can be.*
>
> Romans 8:6-7

If God says you're healed, the mind will say what the doctor has said. It will insist, "I am sick." As proof, the mind will remind you constantly of the pain you are feeling in your body. But God said, *"Himself took our infirmities, and bare our sicknesses"* (Matthew 8:17). He has already spoken to your spirit. If your spirit catches it and believes it, it will then attempt to send a message to your mind. However, your mind is no doubt blocked.

In Old Testament times, Elisha, a man of God, predicted, "By this time tomorrow there will be a surplus of goods" (see 2 Kings 7:1). When men in charge of finances hear that, they automatically respond, "It can't happen." This shows why politicians can never solve your problems. Wall Street also does not have the answer. Only the One who sits on the throne can give you the answers you need.

You have received the mind of Christ, and this means that the same wisdom that was in Jesus is now in you. But, in order to operate at that level, you must step into the Spirit realm.

Your spirit knows everything Jesus knows. All that you need to do is to consult your spirit. How can you do that? Speak in tongues and ask God, "What are You saying?" He will drop something into your spirit because your spirit is linked to Him.

> *But ye have an unction from the Holy One, and ye know all things.*
> 1 John 2:20

You cannot fail if you listen to the Spirit of God. However, if you've already made up your mind, God can't help you. Through the anointing of God, you can access any and all knowledge that you need.

When God said, *"ye know all things,"* He was not talking about your small brain. You know all things in your spirit, and nothing comes that will embarrass you. You have the mind of Christ.

An angel of the Lord appeared to John. When he saw the angel, John's first instinct was to worship him, but the angel told him not to do that:

> *And I John saw these things, and heard them. And when I had heard and seen, I fell down to worship before the feet of the angel which shewed me these things. Then saith he unto me, See thou do it not: for I am thy fellowservant, and of thy brethren the prophets, and of them which keep the sayings of this book: worship God.* Revelation 22:8-9

The angel told John not to worship him because they were in the same category. Both were spirits:

> *And of the angels he saith, Who maketh his angels spirits, and his ministers a flame of fire.* Hebrews 1:7

God's ministering spirits are angels. Therefore, it was a spirit that talked with John, and since we are in the same category, the angel was not to be worshiped.

It seems clear that John didn't know who this angel was, and we, too, need to get acquainted with our spirits. Our spirits live in the same house as our mind and body, but they are not well acquainted. Believe it or not, your body doesn't know the real you, and neither does your mind. Therefore, you must not allow them to lead you.

The sad thing is that you need them. You can't survive on this earth without them. Your spirit doesn't walk on the street; it needs a body to carry it around. And your mind is the valve through which information passes before it can be transferred to your body.

Your spirit gives information to your mind, and your mind sends the message to your body. When Mr. Body says, "I am weak," Mr. Mind agrees. "You've worked so hard! No wonder you're weak!" The spirit, however, does not agree. It says, "How can we be weak? The joy of the Lord is our strength. Let the weak say, 'I am strong.'"

The mind is relentless, hammering away at the body, telling it how weak it is. If there is no intervention, before long this man will be telling everyone around him how tired he feels.

Since the real you can never be weak, how do we fix this? We just need to hear what the Word of God says, because the Word of God is the food of the spirit and the voice of the spirit. When the Word comes into your spirit, and you keep saying it with your mouth, your mind can pick up on it.

*Therefore let no man glory in men. For all things are yours; whether Paul, or*

*Apollos, or Cephas, or the world, or life, or death, or things present, or things to come; all are yours.*

1 Corinthians 3:21-22

We must not be proud and follow the "wise men" of this world. The Lord has given you all that you need. Life and death are your servants. When you step into the spirit world, even death can't embarrass you.

Go ahead, take that step. That's where you belong. Then you can speak to your body and say, "Cancer die now! You can't stay here! Get out in Jesus' name!"

Your empowerment as a spirit man is by the Word of God and the name of Jesus. When you connect to the spirit realm in this way, you will be able to pull down all the forces of Hell. Life, death, and all demons are under you.

Sadly, many people do not like the Word of God. His Word works, but many fail to work His Word. Because they have no time for it, preferring to spend their time pampering the flesh or feeding the mind, the Word doesn't produce for them.

But how can you have faith without the Word of God? This is the same faith Jesus, Paul, and the other apostles used. Why, then, will it not work for you? Could it be that the reason it doesn't work for you is that you have no time for it?

When you don't have the Word in you, the devil can slap you at will. That is why I refuse to preach fifteen-minute messages as many do. God has sent me to preach Truth, and that takes longer. I am always aware that my preaching will not appeal to everyone, but I can't help that.

For those who are willing to pay the price, I am able to put in their mouths what is in me. Then the devil cannot embarrass them. As James wrote:

> *Thou believest that there is one God; thou doest well: the devils also believe, and tremble.*                James 2:19

You and I are in the same class with Jesus, and it was grace that brought us to this point. None of us did anything to merit it, and you don't need to kill yourself trying to get there. Simply believe the Word and act on it. The Bible says:

> *In whom ye also trusted, after that ye heard the word of truth, the gospel of your salvation: in whom also after that ye believed, ye were sealed with that holy Spirit of promise.*     Ephesians 1:13

God has sealed your spirit so that it cannot be contaminated. Let that Spirit affect your mind, your finances, your speech, everything about you. If you remain carnal, you won't be able to live a holy life or to tithe as God requires. Therefore, the Lord is speaking to your spirit. That's the only way you can be blessed.

Never allow your mind to prevail over your spirit. The Spirit of God is so gentle. He will remain quiet if you become carnal. The Bible says:

*For he that will love life, and see good days, let him refrain his tongue from evil, and his lips that they speak no guile.* 1 Peter 3:10

There are people who, when they open their mouth, only gossip comes out. What should come from your mouth? Whatever the Spirit is saying, agree with it. Forget about how you feel, and don't bother to tell everyone about it. Talk about what edifies.

Don't stagnate other people's destiny by telling them bad things about themselves, and be careful who you reveal your dreams to. Joseph revealed the secrets of his life to his enemies (his own brothers), and the result was that he went through a terrible experience. Despite it all, God brought his dreams to pass, but he had to go through a lot of pain he would not have had to endure otherwise.

In case you don't know it yet, God's Word is the Spirit realm for every believer. There is no demon, principality, sickness, or power that is able to stand against you when you are full of God's Word. Everything the Lord made He put under your feet as you believe Him and act on His Word.

We have been sealed with the Holy Spirit of God, the Lord has given us to Jesus, and no one will be able to pluck us out of His hands. Sickness, oppression, and poverty cannot separate us from God:

> *My Father, which gave them me, is greater than all; and no man is able to pluck them out of my Father's hand.* John 10:29

Your spirit cannot be dislodged. However, your mind can be dislodged if you expose it to carnal movies or online smut. Such things can and do unleash the activities of demons, principalities, and powers. If you've been watching vampire movies, for example, when people come close, you may wonder if they perhaps want to suck your blood. The mind is susceptible to so many lies.

The Spirit realm is the place of the Word of God. When you are born again and armed with the Word of God, you are no longer an ordinary person. You're are like Christ in this world. Through this position, you have authority over everything.

Jesus lives in you. There was a time when Jesus was tired and hungry, but on the inside He was still God:

> *It is the spirit that quickeneth; the flesh profiteth nothing: the words that I speak unto you, they are spirit, and they are life.* John 6:63

When it was time to address any issue, Jesus commanded demons to get out. It's time for you to step into who you are in Christ. Please declare this: "I am in Christ!"

Remember, you didn't work for it. Grace brought you to it. You are in Christ, and since you are in Christ, everything must work for you.

Since you are in Christ, favor must come to you. Since you are in Christ, no negative situation will prevail over you. By the Word of God and through the name of Jesus, you will prevail over all.

Learn to stand on the Word of God, and speak to the situations in your life. Command sickness to get out of your body. Command every part of your body to be renewed in Jesus' name. Declare, "I receive brand new parts for all the vital organs of my body in Jesus' name." Don't consider what you are saying with your mind. The Word of God is powerful, and it works.

One day Jesus commanded a fig tree to wither, and you can do unusual miracles like that too if you have the same kind of faith.

The real you is in Christ, so don't be deceived. Don't let anyone or anything deceive you. Step into your place in Christ Jesus. Walk in the consciousness that you are in Christ. Stand in that place and begin to decree favor over your life.

Toward the end of His time on Earth, Jesus told His disciples to go into the city and untie a donkey and her colt they would encounter there. They were to bring them to Him.

Jesus had the audacity to do this because He was the Lord who ruled over everything, including the owner of those donkeys. Whenever you open your month, it's no more you, but Jesus speaking through you. So, make your declarations in faith.

The disciples wondered what they should say if someone questioned them about taking the donkey. Jesus told them to say: *"The Lord hath need of them"* (Matthew 21:3). As soon as they heard that, Jesus indicated, *"straightway he will send them"* (same verse).

Sure enough, when someone saw the disciples and asked, "What are you doing there?" the disciples answered, "We came to get these donkeys for the Lord," and that person answered, "Okay!" There were no more questions asked. What Jesus said was sure and could not fail.

Jesus said He would never leave us nor forsake us. Therefore, God is with you. Declare that! Speak it forth, and do it as if you know it.

I decree right now in the name of Jesus Christ that you will excel. You will fulfill your destiny. No power from the pit of Hell will be able to subdue you in Jesus' name. Now, that is *Heaven on Earth*.

# CHAPTER 19

# THE PROMISE OF THE SPIRIT THROUGH FAITH

*Christ hath redeemed us from the curse of the law, being made a curse for us: for it is written, Cursed is every one that hangeth on a tree: that the blessing of Abraham might come on the Gentiles through Jesus Christ; that we might receive the promise of the Spirit through faith.*                Galatians 3:13-14

Who you are and what you are capable of doing in Christ Jesus is massive. The enemy has lied to you about who you are. There's no reason why men and women in Christ should be sick, poor, or afflicted, or should fail. Man was created in the same class with God, so we are a replica of the Almighty.

> *And God said, Let us make man in our image, after our likeness: and let them have dominion over the fish of the sea, and over the fowl of the air, and over the cattle, and over all the earth, and over every creeping thing that creepeth upon the earth.* Genesis 1:26

The word *image* means "a picture of the original." There was nothing in God that was not in Adam. When man fell and died (he fell spiritually and later died physically), God made an amendment by sending Jesus Christ to rebirth our spirit, to recreate it, so that we would look like His Son.

There's no reason why you should be complaining about what the devil is doing in your life because you're in charge. The Bible says that we are heirs of God and joint heirs with Jesus Christ. You are joined with the Lord, making you one spirit with Him.

*What? know ye not that he which is joined to an harlot is one body? For two, saith he, shall be one flesh. But he that is joined unto the Lord is one spirit.*

1 Corinthians 6:16-17

You are one spirit with the Lord. This means that what Jesus is capable of doing you can also do (see John 14:12). When you don't take the Scriptures as God speaking directly to you, that's a problem. You can believe your credit card or your pin number when you use your ATM card, but would you doubt God's Word?

Which is more reliable, God's Word or our credit system? The last time I checked, computers still made mistakes, but God never does. If He says you're rich, then you're rich.

God says you are blessed, so why are you complaining? He says you are joined with His Son and that you are one spirit with Him. The secret of Jesus is not who He was when He walked in the streets of Jerusalem. His secret was what the Father said about Him.

This man called Jesus began His life on Earth in a manger in the midst of the animals, but He knew inside of Himself that He was God. God has said that you are created in the likeness of His Son. You are joined together with Him, and you can do the works that He did.

Do you believe in Jesus, that He died and rose again? His mandate has not changed. God means what He says, and He has enough power to back up everything He says. All too often, what the enemy succeeds in doing is to show you who you are *not*. He convinces you by showing you what you're passing through in life, especially the things your eyes can see. His goal is to reduce you to flesh and blood and education.

Satan lies to you that you are just a man with a body and a soul. He never talks about your spirit, for he knows that when you discover you are not just a man walking through this life in your body and going to that school or doing whatever you do on a daily basis, everything will change. He knows that when you realize you are in the same class with Almighty God, nothing will ever be the same again. He knows you will tell him to shut his mouth, and he doesn't want you to get to that level of understanding.

You don't have to be a pastor to operate at this level. The day you got saved, God gave you the same grace He gave to His Son, Jesus. I know that religious people don't like to hear this because they think it's "just too much," but it's the truth of the Word. You can't tear it out of the Bible. You may tear it out of yours, but we refuse to tear it out of ours. It's the truth, and truth will stand forever.

Please declare, "I am in the same class with God through my Lord Jesus Christ. I know it, and I am taking authority right now in the name of Jesus." If you believe it and declare it, the enemy will be forced to flee.

If poverty and disease didn't harass Jesus, there's no reason why they should torment you. The psalmist had a wonderful revelation. He said:

> *What is man, that thou art mindful of him? and the son of man, that thou visitest him? For thou hast made him a little lower than the angels, and hast crowned him with glory and honour. Thou madest him to have dominion over the works of thy hands; thou hast put all things under his feet.*     Psalm 8:4-6

The word *angel* here means "Elohim," the Creator of all things. Please declare, "All things are under my feet." Believe it and declare it, and it will be so. Don't let the devil reduce you to a thing. Don't let him reduce you to your academic qualifications or to your place of employment. You're more than that. Don't let him reduce you to the car you drive or the house you live in. There's a greater dimension of you that he cannot see. Everything Jesus Christ is capable of doing you can also do.

God created you to have dominion, and has put all things under your feet. Your mind can't understand this because it will reason God out of the picture.

God is talking to your spirit because your spirit looks like Jesus and has no sin, no blemish whatsoever. Your spirit has all the intelligence, all the anointing, and all the glory. Paul said it this way:

> *Therefore if any man be in Christ, he is a new creature: old things are passed away; behold, all things are become new.* 2 Corinthians 5:17

What man is God talking about? It's the man on the inside of you. The good news is that the man on the inside of you controls everything around you.

Not so long ago, I had a situation in which my cellphone began to malfunction while we were at a retreat. Before long, it was completely dead. I called to one of my associates and asked what we could do? I had been scheduled to have a phone meeting with that faulty phone.

When I got back home, I was meditating on who I am. I thought about Jesus. What would He have done if His phone had

223

died? Wouldn't He be calling on the angels to come and help Him? So, I said, "Phone, you've got to work—now."

As I stood there, determined to take this victory, the Spirit of the Lord spoke to me and said, "You can do it if you want." Then the Lord said, "Stand on it." Don't reduce yourself to the way other people see you. The mirror you're looking at every morning is just a physical reflection of yourself. When you see the Word, you will see who you really look like.

I put that phone on the floor, stood on it, and said, "Thank You, Jesus," and the phone began to work again. Could anyone explain the technology behind that? In the same way, I declare over your life today that every oppression is destroyed. I declare over your life that every limitation is destroyed.

If God can heal a cellphone, then He can heal your finances, He can heal your body, and He can heal your marriage. Your destiny is perfected right now. When situations arise, step out of your limitations. Look at the situation and make a prophetic declaration to change it.

God wants you to prosper. That's why He redeemed you from the curse of the Law. Unfortunately, most people think prosperity is all about money. Take prosperity out of your redemption, and there would be nothing left. It's all part of the bundle:

> *Beloved, I wish above all things that thou mayest prosper and be in health, even as thy soul prospereth.* 3 John 1:2

You are so loved that there exists a plan for your prosperity. God wants you to prosper spiritually and financially. When you prosper spiritually, it is because you are born again. Your spirit is reconnected with its Maker.

You prosper in your mind when you have the wisdom of God. You prosper financially when you have enough money to share with others and to use for the glory of God's name. Prosperity is not just for you; you are to use it to prosper God's Kingdom.

You prosper in body when you are healthy. Prosperity is not all about money. That's a part of it, but it's not the totality of what Christ redeemed you for. When He redeemed you, He pulled you out of every curse, and poverty is part of that curse.

The curse of the Law came because someone broke the Law. If you break the Law, the curse comes. The Bible says, *"For all have sinned, and come short of the glory of God"* (Romans 3:23). There is no one who merits God's blessing, no one who merits His glory. Why? We have been cut short because of the sin man committed in the Garden of Eden. But the Bible shows that Jesus Christ came and took that curse upon Himself. He became a curse so that you and I can have the blessing.

So, what's our problem? It's insanity to try to pay for what you can't afford. God saw our state, our desperation, to get to the root level, and He made provision for our prosperity by sending Jesus Christ. He became a curse, so that we could receive the blessings of Abraham. That blessing was material:

*For the promise, that he should be the heir of the world, was not to Abraham, or to his seed, through the law, but through the righteousness of faith.*

Romans 4:13

Do not depend on your job to live. There is so much God wants to do for and through you. *The New Living Translation* of the Bible says it this way:

*Clearly, God's promise to give the whole earth to Abraham and to His descendants was not based on his obedience to God's law, but on a right relationship with God that comes by faith.*

Abraham didn't do anything to earn this blessing. If it was because he offered Isaac, then each of us would need to kill our own Isaac to become righteous. God is not dealing with you because you are good; He's dealing with you because Jesus is good.

Jesus is the One who paid the price that moved the Father. God will do anything under the heavens because of Jesus. It's not because you're the best in town. God loves you, but not because you're lovely. God will do anything because He loves Jesus, and Jesus has already paid your price.

From the moment you got saved, God deals with you as if He's dealing with Jesus, His own Son. All of your faults are covered with His blood, and He cannot see beyond the blood.

There was a time when Balaam was offered money to curse the children of Israel, and when a curse is placed on you, poverty follows. It's automatic. The man took the money and was ready to curse Israel, but there was a sacrifice in the camp — the blood of bulls and goats — and God cannot overlook the power of the blood.

As Balaam was about to curse the children of Israel, God told him that he could not curse them because they were blessed by Him (see Numbers 22:12).

In the following chapter of Numbers, Balaam explained:

*God is not a man, that he should lie; neither the son of man, that he should repent: hath he said, and shall he not do it? or hath he spoken, and shall he not make it good? Behold, I have received commandment to bless: and he hath blessed; and I cannot reverse it. He hath not beheld iniquity in Jacob, neither hath he seen perverseness in Israel: the LORD his God is with him, and the shout of a king is among them.*

Numbers 23:19-21

There were indeed iniquities which the people had committed, but God said He didn't see them (even though they had done them). When the blood steps in, your faults are removed. God said:

*For I will be merciful to their unrighteousness, and their sins and their iniquities will I remember no more.*

Hebrews 8:12

That's enough! The enemy wants to bring you back to your past so that he can limit what God can do in your life. That's why he tries to keep you under guilt and fear. But if you trust that it's true that Jesus Christ died and rose from the dead, then why not believe for everything He provided through that sacrifice? Why take only the righteousness and leave the rest? He has given unto us *"all things that pertain unto life and godliness"* (2 Peter 1:3).

If you don't understand now, you may get to Heaven, but you will be remain confused down here. God doesn't want you to be heavenly conscious but earthly useless. He has provided everything you will ever need for victory in this life through the death, resurrection, and ascension of our Lord Jesus Christ.

God wants you to know that Jesus has already paid for everything you will ever need to prosper. I will not pray for you to be blessed. I will remind you that you have *already been blessed*. The status of your spirit is the same as the status of Jesus Christ:

> *No man hath seen God at any time. If we love one another, God dwelleth in us, and his love is perfected in us.*   1 John 4:12

If we have lived like Jesus Christ here on this Earth, we will not be afraid of the Judgment. You and I are in Christ Jesus. I didn't say that; God said it.

> *As he is, so are we in this world.*
>                                             1 John 4:17

Not as He *was*, but as He *is* in His resurrection glory. "*As he is, so we are in this world.*" Therefore, I can look at death, cancer, and diabetes and command them to get out of my life in Jesus' name, and they will obey. This is not true because of who I am, but because of what Jesus has done.

Again, the problem we have in the Body of Christ is that our mind and body haven't yet met the real us. We are living in the same house, but we don't know each other. We eat together and sleep together, but we have never met, and we're not listening to what our spirit is saying. We are only looking at what the Internet and our educational qualifications are telling us.

In school, I was taught that we breathe in oxygen and breathe out carbon dioxide, and that is what gives us life. But years later I discovered that the Bible tells it differently:

*And the* LORD *God formed man of the dust of the ground, and breathed into his nostrils the breath of life; and man became a living soul.* Genesis 2:7

When I read that, I said, "Thank You, Lord, for giving me life." That life is in me to destroy all manner of darkness:

*And the light shineth in darkness; and the darkness comprehended it not.* John 1:5

There was a lady in our church from Ethiopia whose little boy, two years old, had never started walking. She always carried him because she didn't want anyone to know that he couldn't walk.

The Lord said to me, "Touch his legs, and when you touch him, My life will flow through you." I touched his leg and said,

"In the name of Jesus, walk." That night, as they were all sleeping, the boy jumped down from his bed and woke the mother up.

The grace of God is bringing you results now. Your miracle will come knocking on your door. Everything you will ever need has been provided by grace. The problem many have is this: grace may set the table, but faith takes a seat.

David sang:

> *Thou preparest a table before me in the presence of mine enemies: thou anointest my head with oil; my cup runneth over.* Psalm 23:5

Anything you'll ever need in life is on that table. Grace has already provided it. You cannot be asking God to provide what He's already done. Too many people fast and pray about things that are already theirs. God has already provided it. You just need to exercise your faith and receive it.

God is not going to heal you in some future. You are already healed. However, you need faith to appropriate your healing. Don't let the devil tell you you're not worthy. If you want your mind to meet with your spirit, then meditate on the Word of God.

If you want your mind to know who you really are, renew it with the Word of God. That's why I pity people who don't read the Scriptures and don't attend anointed worship services. They are looking for miracles, but they don't know how to get them.

You shouldn't have to be looking for miracle. Miracles should be looking for you. You were born for signs and wonders. That's your make-up. You were destined to make declarations and see things start happening. If you don't know this, nothing will happen.

*For the grace of God that bringeth salvation hath appeared to all men.*

Titus 2:11

There is not one person on Earth for whom God did not settle salvation. We are all candidates for salvation, but not all of us release our faith to get it. It does not come by works. God's part is grace, and your part is faith.

Faith doesn't necessarily move God; it moves you. God is already moved; Jesus has moved God. Now you're the one who needs to move, so that you can access what God has already provided.

If you are not getting what you need and desire out of life, it is not because God has not healed or blessed you. It is your faith you should work on to get you what already belongs to you.

The glory around you is so great. Job was dying of fear, yet God had placed a hedge around him. Job couldn't see it, but the devil saw it.

You don't know how strong the fence is that God has made around you. The devil is saying, "I can't get in," while you are speaking doubt. If you know that Jesus died and rose from the dead, why don't you believe what He said? He brought about your full salvation. Why are you doubting?

If you are doubting, then you don't believe that He rose. If you know that He rose and that He's still alive, then what's your problem? The race of faith is to depend on the finished work of Christ, not in your ability or effort. Try as you might, you cannot earn salvation for yourself.

The reason many don't tithe and sow seeds of giving is that they don't believe that Jesus Christ rose from the dead. They may consent to it, but do they actually believe it with their whole heart? The race of faith believes the Word. If it's in the Word, you go to bed in peace, knowing that God will take care of it.

As we have seen, the greatest labor God requires of you is to labor to rest. Because I know that I am so loved, I don't need to be concerned about anything. My heavenly Father will take care of it, and so it's not my business.

Father God healed me already. Because I don't doubt that He rose from the dead, I have been redeemed. I don't need to think about it. It is done:

> *Grace be to you and peace from God the Father, and from our Lord Jesus Christ, who gave himself for our sins, that he*

*might deliver us from this present evil world, according to the will of God and our Father.* Galatians 1:3-4

God's will is that I am delivered from this present world. Don't be afraid of what the devil wants to do to you, because Christ has already delivered you from it through the work of the cross.

The more ignorant you are of these truths the more oppression you will suffer from Satan. God said:

*My people are destroyed for lack of knowledge.* Hosea 4:6

Let today mark the end of every oppression in your life. God is opening a new chapter for you. I command every place where the world has closed against you to open for you right now in the name of Jesus Christ.

The Macedonian church changed the story of their lives because they knew the right key to press. The Bible says they were poor, as we say, "So poor the poor called them poor." But the grace of God came upon them. They understood that we cannot earn anything by our efforts. Stirred by the grace of God, they began to give out of their deep poverty, according to their ability, and beyond their ability, and Heaven opened over them.

You are not poor because you don't have a job; you are poor because you are not sowing enough seed. God responds to seed, not to your tears, not to your job. He responds to your seed as you are stirred by the Spirit. When you experience that stirring, don't wait for someone to ask you to give. Take a step of faith, and see what God will do.

As noted before, in most parts of the world, there are seasons for planting certain crops. When it's time to plant corn, if you are away travelling, when you come back, the time for planting may be past. And, if you plant at the wrong time, you cannot expect a hundredfold return.

If you were supposed to take an exam and, instead, you present a doctor's report that you were sick, will you be promoted anyway? No, you will eventually have to sit for the exam.

The devil is attacking your finances because there's no seed, and the reason you don't plant seed is that you don't believe with all your heart that Jesus Christ is risen from the dead.

If someone said to you, "Give me a one-dollar bill, and I will give you one hundred dollars in exchange," you would give it quickly. The Bible says:

> *And every one that hath forsaken houses, or brethren, or sisters, or father, or mother, or wife, or children, or lands, for my name's sake, shall receive an hundredfold, and shall inherit everlasting life.*                 Matthew 19:29

Peter changed his life with a seed. He had toiled all night and caught nothing. Then, the next morning, he gave Jesus his boat. After Jesus used the boat to preach, He told Peter, *"Launch out into the deep"* (Luke 5:4).

Peter gave Jesus his boat, and Jesus gave Peter so many fish that his net broke.

God didn't take the boat away from Peter. Instead, with this one miraculous catch, Peter was able to retire. From that day forward, he never lacked. One seed and one catch led to his retirement, and he never needed to work again.

Instead, Peter now went out as a missionary, celebrating the goodness of Jesus Christ all over the world. As you respond to the seed, grace makes you rich, and your seed is a proof of your response. Men won't make you rich; they won't bring you money. Peter said to Jesus, *"We have toiled all the night, and have taken nothing: nevertheless at thy word I will let down the net"* (Luke 5:5).

Then Peter put his net back into the water, and suddenly all the fish in the lake found their way into it. From today, people will start running after you. I release upon you right now the favor of God that you need to fulfill His mandate upon your life.

There's no reason on earth why your story cannot change. The principle of the Word of God is that Heaven and Earth will pass away but not one word of what God has said will be wasted (see Mark 13:31).

I refuse to hoard money and not give it to God because I know I don't own it. God told me many years ago that the secret of my prosperity would lie in me not owning anything. At the point of my need, God shows up because I own nothing.

There's is never a time when God asks me to give something and I have to think about it. Give to God whenever He stirs your heart. Too often, He stirs our hearts, and we shut Him out. When you give, that's the only way He can bless you.

There's a principle in the Kingdom that gives you what you want. Speak to your life. I decree over you now, "In the name of Jesus Christ, move forward. I clear every obstacle in your path in Jesus' name."

It's your time to move to the next level. I decree: "You are healed, and you are blessed." I decree over your life that all your needs are met. There's no longer any limitation in your life in Jesus' name. Now, that is *Heaven on Earth*.

# CHAPTER 20

# In Conclusion

*Every good gift and every perfect gift
is from above, and cometh down from
the Father of lights, with whom is no
variableness, neither shadow of turning.*

James 1:17

It is in and through the Word of God that
we get our victory, our success, and our
strength. His Word teaches us that in the
original plan, the Earth was programmed
and patterned after Heaven. Yes, this dark-
ened planet was originally patterned after
God's own dwelling place.

Life on Earth was never meant to be
independent of Heaven, since Heaven is
the source of all strength and provision.

Therefore, if you can reconnect with the original Source, you will have no difficulty living on this Earth successfully.

Every good and perfect gift comes down from the Father of lights. Why? Because *He* is the Source of everything that pertains to life and godliness. When Jesus Christ came here, He began to show people that there is no need for us to be stagnated, to be frustrated, to be useless upon the Earth. There is provision, and it will be activated the moment you come into God's Kingdom, by giving your life to Jesus.

There is enough provision for all of life's necessities. Jesus taught us to pray:

> *After this manner therefore pray ye: our father which art in heaven, hallowed be thy name. Thy kingdom come thy will be done in earth as it is in heaven.*
>
> Matthew 6:9-10

With this, Jesus began to show His disciples that there was no reason for them to struggle in life. Since they had chosen to serve Him, the Father's will could be done on Earth exactly as it was in Heaven. If what you are experiencing right now is not what Heaven experiences, then you have every right to question it.

Far too many believers just go to church because it's Sunday, and that is the place to be. Sadly, many believers go to church filled with questions about why life is not working out for them. There are things in their life that are not supposed to be there, and the things that are supposed to be there are somehow missing.

Well, one thing is sure: when you go to church, you have gone to the right place. There, in the presence of God, you can reconnect with the Source of all things, the Source of the very things you are looking for.

Jesus could not and cannot lie, and He said that the Father's will can be done in Earth as it is in Heaven. This means that we should be living in *Heaven on Earth*.

If something in your life is not in the order of Heaven, there is a malfunction somewhere that needs to be corrected. We have, the Scriptures assure us, everything that pertains to life and godliness:

> *Grace and peace be multiplied unto you through the knowledge of God, and of Jesus our Lord, according as his divine power hath given unto us all things that pertain unto life and godliness, through the knowledge of him that hath called us to glory and virtue: whereby are given unto us exceeding great and precious promises: that by these ye might be partakers of the divine nature, having escaped the corruption that is in the world through lust.* 2 Peter 1:2-4

The Bible presents a picture of what is obtainable in Heaven and, therefore, should be obtainable right here on Earth, and that is true now in the twenty-first century.

None of us have ever been to Heaven, except by revelation, but you can experience Heaven through Christ, and you can learn what Heaven is like through God's Word.

If what is described and promised in this marvelous Book is not yet found in your life, you have every right to expect it and to seek God for it.

God even authorizes us, as followers of Christ, to decree and demand the manifestation of what He has promised. For instance, by the authority that is in the name of Jesus, we can demand that whatever is due you physically, spiritually, financially, maritally, or academically that is not yet there be released to you today.

With this knowledge, you can go into the Book and learn what you are promised as a child of God. As you do this, faith rises in your heart to act on it and receive it.

We are not just playing religion when we go to church. We are building the Kingdom of our God and learning to live by Kingdom principles.

Many believers, when they suffer lack, excuse it by saying that God is just training them. That is absurd. Training you for what? Is He training you in poverty? How can you give what you don't have? There is no poverty in Heaven, so if you are experiencing poverty, it has originated with the wicked one, not with God.

There is no disease in Heaven, so how could God be training you to suffer disease? There is no fear in Heaven, so God cannot possibly be training you in the art of fear? When you become convinced in your heart that God loves you totally and that everything in His Word is for you and you should have it, you will quickly become established.

Far too many people who come to God have the mindset that they will have to struggle for what they need. No! You do not have to struggle! Everything has been provided for you, and God has given you those things as an inheritance.

It might surprise some to know that among the many cultures of this diverse Earth I have not found a single case of someone having to pay for their inheritance. This idea only exists in the minds of those who are deceived.

Yes, I know there are many different teachings about God from pulpits around the world. This is the reason you need to learn what God says for yourself. Don't take someone else's word for it. Search it out. You owe it to your soul. You owe it your spouse, your children, and your grandchildren. Don't risk losing the blessing of God because of rumors or traditions.

Here's what God says about you:

> *For I know the thoughts that I think toward you, saith the* Lord*, thoughts of peace, and not of evil, to give you an expected end.* Jeremiah 29:11

Again, peace has nothing to do with quietness. When God said peace, He was talking about *shalom*, which means nothing missing and nothing broken. He was talking about wholeness. That is your inheritance, and you don't have to work for it.

If a parent or grandparent has made a will, what would qualify you to receive something from their estate? Just because you live close to their house? Just because you have known them for a long time? No, it is because you are their child or grandchild. This inheritance is not anything you worked for, and remember, you are a child of the Most High God.

God said He has a plan for you, and in that plan is nothing evil. Therefore, anything that is not part of the plan of God for your life has no right standing with you.

God has stated who He is, who you are, and what is yours because you are His, and that settles it. You don't have to fix anything. It has already been fixed by Calvary. Far too many people fail to realize what their true inheritance is in Christ and His Word, and that is why we have so many struggling in life.

There is absolutely no reason for things not to work out for you. You are right now in Heaven by faith in Christ Jesus. Stop interpreting the Word of God with human intelligence. Let God give you His knowledge and wisdom.

Genesis 6:11 recounts the story of a group of people who were so arrogant they decided to build a tower to Heaven to find God. The amazing thing is that they proceeded to spend all their efforts and finances on this project. In the end, God had to stop them. I have no idea how far they got, but I doubt very much if they were able to reach to the thirty-five thousand feet where modern passenger jets fly. Even at that altitude, no one has found God. That can only be done in the Spirit. Heaven is above all things.

God said in His Word:

> *But God, who is rich in mercy, for his great love wherewith he loved us, even when we were dead in sins, hath quickened us together with Christ, (by grace ye are saved;) and hath raised us up together, and made us sit together in heavenly places in Christ Jesus: that in the ages to come he might shew the exceeding riches of his grace in his kindness toward us through Christ Jesus.*
>
> Ephesians 2:4-7

You cannot be sitting in such an amazing place of authority and still be feeling like a victim. It is time to act like who and what you are. You are not a beggar; you are a ruler. You are already seated in heavenly places in Christ Jesus.

Religion has relegated us to slavery, and we must flush out that lie by the knowledge of the truth of God's Word. You are invincible, and you need to understand that. The same force that was in Jesus is in you:

> *Ye are of God, little children, and have overcome them: because greater is he that is in you, than he that is in the world.* 1 John 4:4

Who are the *"them"* referred to here in the first sentence? Those are the forces arrayed against your destiny, but the promise of God is: *"greater is he that is in you, than he that is in the world."* That settles it. You have overcome *"them,"* so, start acting like it.

I didn't write that just for this book. It was written thousands of years ago by God's anointed servant John. This is not a new truth. It has been true ever since Calvary. There is a force inside of you that is greater than the evil forces of the world. Therefore, don't let any situation intimidate you. That situation you are worried about has been afraid that you are coming. It knows who you are. Do you?

You get all these things by releasing your faith in what the Word of God says. We have discovered by the Word of God that faith will not work unless grace has provided it. Faith cannot take what grace has not provided.

If you go into a Walmart store, you will find that they sell almost everything, but you cannot go to a Walmart and say you want to buy a car. Why? Because Walmart has not made any provision for selling vehicles.

In a Super-Walmart, you can buy car parts, groceries, medications, clothing, pet supplies, hardware, and many other things, and you don't need to beg anybody to sell it to you. If you are a regular customer at Walmart, you may already know where to find what you need at any given moment.

Walmart has become such a part of American life that some people, if they haven't been to Walmart that day, feel sick. But you can only buy what Walmart provides.

There are many things that grace has already provided. The last time I checked, grace had already provided all things that pertain to life and godliness. So, your every need is already supplied. You just need to claim it.

You and I ruling this earth was not an idea that any man conceived; it was preordained before the world began. What was in God was put in man so that man could rule the way God would have ruled this Earth. And that has not changed. Yes, you can experience *Heaven on Earth* right here and right now. Why not start today?

# Author Contact
# Information

You may contact the author directly in the following way:

*eMail:* Bishopidowu@crepa.org

*Telephone:* (904) 469-5724